To:
Kristy Blessee
Sacred Thai

A Call To

SACRED LIVING

Stepping into our Divine power... a path to health, peace,
love, joy and harmony for ourselves and our world!

Cynthia Koloup Belden

ISBN 978-1-7355719-0-4 (paperback)
ISBN 978-1-7355719-1-1 (ebook)

Dedication Page

This book is dedicated to my grandmother, Memom, and my mother, Carolyn. Both were my guides as stewards of the sacred path. I feel so blessed to have had them in my life then and in spirit always. My grandmother was a master of sacred living and walked the path of spiritual devotion in grace and faith, even on the day she died at the age of 96. My mother walked the sacred path of spiritual empowerment. She instilled in me strength and courage to live as my authentic sacred self, and encouraged me to use my gifts to serve the world. As she would often say, "to those who have been given much...much is expected."

I give thanks to my many family members for their relentless support of my numerous life adventures and to all who have shared with me, this journey we call, "life on earth." As we teach each other about ourselves and discover truth and what is meaningful; we are mirrors, supporters and teachers for each other, always.

I give thanks to Marcella Matthaei, editor of Right Whale Books, for her editing skills, writing guidance, and for pushing me to put my teachings in book form.

Much thanks to Hannah Porter and Matthew Quann, a young and talented publishing team for their excellent work further editing, formatting, and consulting on self-publishing and printing this book. A big shout out also goes to the many friends who digested the first drafts and offered needed feedback on the helpfulness of the manuscript.

For all who come to read this guide book, may you be filled with the blessings of the sacred way and all of the love, peace, and joy that it bestows on you, and all of those around you and our beloved Planet Earth, our home!!

I close here giving acknowledgment to all of the indigenous people on the planet, who have been the keepers of the sacred teachings, practices and ways for eons of times until this time, when it was foretold….that it was now the time on planet Earth for them to bring forward their sacred teachings to be put out into the world, so that the entirety of humankind could learn of, and practice the sacred ways, so the people could evolve fully back into their sacred selves, assuming the role of sacred stewards of the planet, of their lives, and of the greater good.

To these spiritually powerful and loving sacred wisdom keepers, we will be forever grateful for unconditionally loving and caring for us, the planet and all beings. To honor their legacy, it is time to fulfill the prophecies and answer their prayers, that WE will now hear "the call to sacred living," and heal the planet and ourselves.

A'ho, Mitauye Oyasin A'ho
(we are all related and so it is)

"All over the sky a sacred voice is calling your name."
-BLACK ELK

*"The time has come to merge spirituality into modern life
and to learn how to put sacredness back into our daily lives"*
-THIA

The Foreword

My goal in writing this book was initially to provide some guidance to those seeking to begin, be reminded, or return to living a daily sacred life through the sharing of my path and experiences on my own road to discovering sacred living. In these critical times on the planet, sacred living becomes a moral imperative. We cannot degrade, diminish, or devalue anyone or anything, as all life is connected and sacred in nature. These current times of separation and disrespect for the planet and one another, requires us to revise our way of being. To become more loving, reverent, respectful, responsible, and caring of all creations on the planet. This is the call to sacred living.

Most of my life, I have been on a quest to understand myself, as well as the world, in a sacred way. I first got a taste of sacred cultures in my teens during my Methodist church retreats, when traveling in the rural Appalachian south. I became aware that even though these people were often materially poor, they were spiritually rich in their deep love of nature, and devotion to all things spiritual. This was expressed in their music, prayers, and conversations. In college I lived in the West African bush for several months on a student cultural immersion experience, and quickly became enamored by the sacredness imbued in this cultures' daily rituals of food preparation, socializing, and work. Life was revered, gratitude was constantly given, and deep connection to nature, creation, and each other was ever present.

My early life experiences with these sacred culture bearers, created a deep awareness in me of our connection to everything, everyone and to nature itself, resulting in a greater quality of inner and outer life, a more sacred life. Experiencing all life as connected, inspired me to want that deep sacred connection to be imbued in my life's daily walk. I became devoted to seeking deeper spiritual understanding as to how to realize that reality. I began traveling in all of my free time to visit sacred sites and sacred wisdom keepers. On these trips, I explored cultures that had remained deeply connected to their sacred spiritual lineage. As I learned about their sacred teachings, practices and rituals, I felt love, peace and harmony from these people who had made the mundane life sacred.

All along this journey, I also read about the spiritual traditions and wisdom teachings, ancient and new age, from around the globe. My early years of study started in the sacred Christian teachings and the legacy of love taught by Jesus. I was gifted over the next 40 years of my life, to study and work with many great eastern spiritual teachers, shamans, indigenous medicine men and women, enlightened scientists, and New Age metaphysical teachers that shared with me their sacred ancient wisdom, spiritual knowledge and practices. Some of their teachings are in book form listed at the end of this work.

In between my travels and studies, I worked and lived by the seashores of the east and west coasts of the USA, as well as the Caribbean. It was while living my day-to-day life that I would be able to merge and integrate these master sacred teachings within my own life experiences, eventually creating and anchoring in seven daily sacred practices that serve to enrich my life and bring me greater health, happiness and harmony on my path to sacred living.

In the first part of this book, Section I "A Call to Sacred Living, The Personal Journey" I take you along on seven sacred healing journeys. We will explore and ultimately discover seven paths that reveal the many ways that sacred living imbues us with feeling, knowing and realizing Universal love, wisdom and personal authentic power in our lives. These seven paths are comprised of sacred wisdom teachings, messages, lessons, and practices that are core components to living a sacred life. This section of the book is informational, inspirational and hopefully will ignite you into taking your own healing journey to increase your sacred awareness, connection and practices, putting you on the path to increased self-love, love of all others and the Divine; the ultimate destination.

> *"While we struggle to figure out why we were put here on earth, all*
> *a dog wants is to love and be loved, a powerful lesson for us all."*
> **– DR BERNIE S. SIEGEL**

In Section II, "A Call to Sacred Living, The Personal Journey" Workbook, I provide you with specific practices, processes, prayers and routines that will furnish instructions and insights to guide you through your own daily sacred healing journey to empowerment, spiritual connection and unconditional love. This is a model for healing and expanding into your higher self so that you can grow sacredly. Learning how to make and maintain sacred connection raises your energy frequency and emotional state. This allows you to engage in greater compassionate self-inquiry as a framework for healing and releasing your denser, victim self, so that you can grow and evolve into your lighter, more joy filled sacred self. Daily life becomes the opportunity for practice and nature provides the support. These practices will help you develop a sacred lens that you can use every day to live in a more loving, sacred way. There are also included daily sacred routines to create a new sacred lifestyle.

> *"Come forward, be in unity and harmony with*
> *your real self, God and mankind."*
> **- PAPA BRAY (HAWAIIAN KAHUNA)**

Section III of this book contains a model of practices for community sacred living. There are certain principles, values and behaviors that really increase the sacred nature of any group gathering, imbuing the group with the ability to find and implement sacred solutions to our day to day life challenges. I call my model, Sacred Living Solution Circles. I invite people who gather together as families, friends, in school, community or business groups to employ these practices and perspectives to align themselves with sacred expressions to heal and bond. When the group comes together in greater peace, compassion and unity with one another, a sacred community is created. In sacred community everyone prospers, benefits and thrives.

> *"Humans need cooperative and caring groups to survive and thrive."*
> **- CHARTER FOR COMPASSION**

I hope that by reading and using this book, you will become illuminated on the value of pursuing a sacred life, inspired to seek your own sacred path, informed on a foot print for sacred action and be ignited to walk sacredly every day, on your own and with others!

Introduction

What is sacred living?

To be sacred means to be **blessed, reverent, holy**. In sacredness, we walk through life knowing that we are ALL connected to all of life and to each other. We are each a spark of unique Divine creation and thus are ALL **holy**; each deserving of respect, honor, and love. When we are living life sacredly, we become consciously aware of our experiences each minute, seeing the Divine in everything and in each other. Every experience is an opportunity to learn, grow, connect and sacredly evolve together. We offer gratitude for our life, for all of life and for all of the many **blessings** in our lives every day. We use our free will to choose our perspectives, words, and actions **reverently**, as we co-create, expand and experience life on planet Earth with our fellow brothers, sisters, Mother Earth, Nature and our cosmic comrades; connected always to Source/Creator/God/Great Spirit.

Sacred living is a walk of remembering and remaining a spiritual being, having a human experience. When we focus on the infinite aspect of our being, the vastness of space and magnificence of creation and nature, we begin to experience our connection to everyone and everything. We begin to remember ourselves as sacred beings, where we rewrite the scripts of our lives to reflect our sacred nature. We envision and choose to create a story that reveres ALL life on earth. In this sacred form, we recognize ourselves as caretakers, collaborators, and co-creators of our lives, our communities, the planet, and the Universe.

Sacred living is not often part of modern culture. Most people in modern societies are over focused on their human experience; acquiring their material goods, worrying about what others think of them, bolstering the comforts of their ego or engaging in the drama of life's many crises, traumas, death, and disease. Believing that the outer material world IS the reality, with an interest in the sacred and spiritual arising only when in crisis, or on Sundays is the standard way of life in modern times. Without the sacred lens or perspective, there can be denial of spiritual reality, distraction from developing the inner self and difficulty living life in a balanced and healthy way. This prevents us from recognizing that this thing we casually call life, is actually always a magical and extraordinarily sacred experience.

How do we get started in living life in a sacred way?

We are all quantum entangled and connected and affect each other all the time, whether we like it or not! We start sacred change with ourselves, what we do to ourselves and then, what we do to others. There are daily practices that can take us into the sacred realms of existence, to experience and become the more sacred aspects of ourselves. This book will take you on a journey based on the sacred teachings of the ancient and current wise ones that is framed for you to consume and use as daily living practices to make your life more sacredly alive every day!

When you break old non-sacred patterns and begin to act from a spiritually inspired place, illuminated by sacred wisdom, ignited to be your authentic higher self, inviting in sacred experiences every day, you receive the keys that open the door to begin sacredly living, and your life becomes a walking prayer!

Table Of Contents

Chapter 4

Stepping out of mind and time and staying in pure presence of each moment

Walking guided by your heart using intuition, moving through life synchronistically and organically

I AM PEACEFUL IN PURE PRESENCE

Chapter 5

Uncovering, discovering and expressing your true authentic self

Learning to serve yourself and others simultaneously as purpose.

I AM EMPOWERED SHARING MY UNIQUE SELF

Chapter 6

Focusing on what is working instead of what is not working in your life by choosing to focus on joy not pain.

Being in gratitude and appreciation for all that you have as lessons, opportunities and blessings every day

I AM JOY-FILLED WHEN I FOCUS THERE

Chapter 7

Feeling unconditional love through your divine connection to the Creator/
God/Source/Great Spirit, Mother Nature and the Universe

Staying connected to divine source love energy by receiving the divine
blessings of universal wisdom, unlimited benevolence and infinite possibilities,
which gives us all that we need, all of the time

I AM LOVE WHEN SOURCED SPIRITUALLY

SECTION II

A Call to Sacred Living - The Personal Journey Workbook

• **U**ncover limited blocks and beliefs causing stress

• **R**elease victim patterns and get clarity of purpose

• **N**avigate raising your vibration into joy, peace, and love

• **E**xpand and live in balance, health and harmony

SECTION III

A Call to Sacred Living - The Community Journey
"Sacred Living Solution Circles"

SECTION I

A Call to Sacred Living - The Personal Journey

Seven Paths to Sacred Living
Insights and Practices

"Make time for quiet moments as God whispers and the world is loud"
-GREG OLSON

Chapter 1

SEEK SOLITUDE

Stop spending so much time distracted in
"doing", spend more time in solitude and stillness
so you can create the space to hear your
authentic sacred voice and that of the Source.

I grew up Baltimore County, Maryland, in a beautiful woodsy setting by a sweet, babbling creek. Whenever I had my own free time, I chose to go down to the creek by myself. It is where I often found my insights, my solace and my joy. In my early years, I wasn't conscious of the importance of sitting alone by the creek most every day. I would go out in the morning before school, and then again in the evening at sunset to sit in my beach chair alone and listen to the creek as the sun went down. I recall how easy it was writing songs and plays alone in my sanctuary. I might go there angry or agitated from a challenging day, but I always came out calmer and with more clarity.

I came to fully understand the value and necessity of daily solitude as a sacred path when I went through my first major life crisis. You know those times when everything comes crashing down in your life all at once? Well, I'd gotten married, raised step kids, had a career and then, one day, the bottom dropped out. Within a 6-month period I got divorced, lost my job, and lost my house.

My first few days all alone in the world, except for my animal family, were very uncomfortable. I wanted to distract myself by making phone calls and taking trips to the store, just to keep from thinking about it. On other days, I wanted to stay in bed and do nothing. However, my dogs had other ideas for me. Gradually, as we took our daily walks to the beach, I realized, as I rushed back to the house after each walk, that I did not need to rush anymore, so we stayed longer.

We actually sat at the beach and watched the surf. I did this every day often three times a day. Each day, I stayed longer and longer. Initially each of my thoughts became louder and louder. They first became filled with anger at my situation, blaming others, seeking solutions to save myself, things to do to distract myself, but honestly, the longer I sat and the longer the weeks went on, these thoughts started to reduce in size and content.

A few weeks into this journey, I discovered I was thinking reflectively instead of reactively about my life. It just happened automatically as I spent more time alone. I was moving from the outer to the inner planes of existence. I was starting to see my part in my drama. I began to understand that things happen for a reason and that when one door closed, another door opened. I didn't realize it at the time, but I was getting honest with myself and my situation. My time in solitude was helping me discover deeper truths and to feel guided to trust my new understandings. By taking the time to be alone I could hear the still voice within me, my spiritual self, which then took over and became the new terrain of my mind and heart. As my spiritual self I was able to operate from a higher, more objective and sacred perspective.

> *"When you are in doubt, be still, and wait; when doubt no longer exists for you, then go forward with courage."*
> **-CHIEF WHITE EAGLE**

I would access this still, reflective observer state of being while in contemplation whenever I was alone at the beach for hours at a time. After another few weeks, in between looking for work, I realized how much I liked having this quiet alone time. So much was revealed when I had no one to answer to but me; no one to judge me but me and no distractions. Eventually, I realized that I was not just sitting alone, but was beginning to dialogue with my observer self and the Universe/ God/ Source of creation. A more evolved, Universal perspective was emerging. One that took into account new truths and awareness. The truth that I owned my life choices, that I created my own reality and that I created the mess I was in, and therefore, I could also create my way out of the mess. There was no one to blame. I began to realize that all life experiences were learning and growth opportunities if we held that higher, sacred perspective. I now no longer lived in doubt and questioning. From stillness in solitude, I could see my path forward with a grounded sacred lens full of clarity.

With sacred sight, I was able to see and understand that I had needed to leave my job. I never would have before, because of my overly loyal nature, but I had been terribly bored and unchallenged there. I saw the house loss as a lesson in detachment and trusted that I had the resources and motivation within myself to recreate a safe home for myself, and my dogs. My divorce had been about drifting apart, when one person changes so much and the other does not wish to. All of the "challenging experiences," when seen through the loving eyes of my higher Universal mind and heart, had now become chances to evolve into a new and more sacred me.

I gradually began to feel comfort and secure again, knowing that I had the power and ability to create whatever I needed. This belief allowed me to drop my fears of lack and limitation and to move through life more courageously. I also realized, that time in solitude had been essential for me in order to go deep within my inner domain and ultimately find my highest direction for forward motion for my life.

With renewed clarity, I was ready to start moving back into the world and find a new job, but I remained very aware that I needed to continue to take time to be in solitude every day. It is only in that alone time that we meet our higher, more objective self, and receive the wisdom from the Universal self that arises in that place.

Throughout my life, I will always have deep gratitude for this learning experience; understanding the need to go daily into a sacred space of solitude, therein to become still, to listen, hear and release my victim self, my stories of blame. By doing this I could go back out into the world and move forward more grounded, with clarity and capability to create a more Divinely empowered reality for myself and those around me.

*"Sit in meditation for twenty minutes every day and if you
are too busy, then you should sit for one hour."*
-OLD ZEN ADAGE

SACRED LIVING PATH #I

MESSAGE: Solitude is necessary

LESSON: Constant "doing,", distractions and busyness keeps us from intimate relationship with ourselves.

PRACTICES: Take time to be alone, be still and listen for the deeper truth within. Release your "victim story," and blaming; become more objective.

Our day-to-day life in the Western world is all about "DOING,". Throughout the day, we mostly spend our time socially interacting or working and reacting to one another's needs and obligations; forgetting our own reflective needs and insight. In order to have a higher quality of life, we must call our energy back from all outside influences and sit alone in peace, recharging, and discovering our internal wisdom.

When we experience the benefits of solitude time, we will feel more comfortable there and we will choose to spend more time there and eventually build in solitude time proactively into our day to day life. This is the foundation and is a necessary practice for living a sacred life.

Start by committing to spending time alone every day, even if it's just for a few minutes. The goal should be an hour a day whenever possible. Choose a quiet place in surroundings that relax you; a meditation room, garden, patio, park bench, or private room in your home. During that time alone, be still and allow your thoughts to rise and fall with your breath. Do not bring judgment to any of them. Learn to observe them. Listen to what they tell you. As your stories of victim-hood and blame take hold, listen to them, feel them fully, get the message, then learn the lesson, and let them go! As you let go of your old stories of blame, fear, lack, and limitation, you release the pain and emotions that accompany those stories. Day-by-day, your human story diminishes and your spiritual sense of inner peace increases. New thoughts arise to fill the empty spaces. Inspiring thoughts about creative ways to move your life forward will come into your mind, with guidance on ways to make yourself happy. Anchor in this new, more spiritual version of yourself, and begin to feel secure in the knowing that you also co- create with the Universe/God; and that all will be well. Set the intention every day during your solitude time, to see, think, and act with higher vision and a spiritual perspective.

"We come in as spirit
the same at the end
the Mystery tells us again and again.
Embodied creation, endless and free,
to choose our life lens
we just need to see.
that in that space, solitude
awakens the view, to everything
waiting for me and for you."
-THIA

I am clear in solitude.

"Collect moments, not things"
- UNKNOWN

Chapter 2

SAVOR SIMPLICITY

Release your <u>attachment</u> to material
things, learn to do with less.
Do less, to have more time to live life freely
Don't rush, go with the flow and let
life unfold easily and effortlessly.

In the north we always had a basement. It was the place to put your extras; extra clothes, furniture, refrigerators, tools. As a child, I found it to be a scary place with generally no windows, or much light, and chaotically cluttered. I never wanted to go down there. My brother and I used to have to go together whenever we were sent to get something from the basement at night. It was as if all of the "stuff," was alive and trying to smother me.

As an adult, in my early years, I'd fill each one of my basements up with all kinds of things that never even got looked at until I moved. I remember the pain of sorting and packing each time I relocated; going through the tons of unnecessary items that I had purchased, in order to give my life supposed meaning, or enjoyment. Let's get real; humans love to shop and acquire in the Western world. It's a cultural meme that stimulates our capitalist economies and it makes us temporarily feel good. Then we move and it gets seen for the burden it is; the credit we owe on it, the time spent cleaning it, the stress at work to pay for it. Stuff wears us down on the back-end, just for the short-term fix of a happy moment or fun experience.

I was at the peak of owning "stuff," when I moved to a Caribbean island in the USVI to simplify my life and to open a spiritual retreat center. Before moving, I had to furnish a 6000 sq. ft villa from stateside. I spent endless days and nights rushing around shopping at discount stores, thrift stores, and garage sales looking for bargains on quality household items. By the time I moved, I had an entire container full. It would take 3-4 weeks for it all to reach my new home, for my simple new island life.

Once I arrived at the villa, during the first week, I settled in and made do with a few chairs and tables, plates and forks, and a simple bed and dresser in the room I was sleeping in. These things had been left by the previous owner. By the second week, with no furnishings to clean and no business yet to manage, I was moving through the days so simply with lots of free time to meditate, explore, and reflect. I loved having so much time alone! I would sit for hours watching hummingbirds visit the multitude of hibiscus flowers on my front veranda. I would float in the pool and gaze up at the sky, watching the amazing cloud formations dance and shift. My body relaxed so deeply that at times, I wondered if I was even in my body. I would wander around the old gardens with my dog smelling the fragrant oleander and jasmine trees that took me back to my travels in India. Time stood still there and nature prevailed. I was already on island time, and loving the deep sense of simplicity and freedom of a life more connected to nature than things.

Then came moving day! The container was on its way from the shipping terminal and my material world came back into play. As the five moving trucks drove up the hill it was suddenly so clear to me that my new-found feeling of inner freedom, and simplicity was due to my material freedom. The few things that I had, had in the place were all that I had needed and enough to make me happy. I keenly saw the beauty and blessings of a minimally material life – Without all the stuff to buy and care for, you can so easily spend your free time going with the flow, and letting life unfold deeply and sacredly. Simplicity was key!

As the boxes started piling up, I began to feel agitated and stressed just thinking about having all of these things around me to take care of again. In just three short weeks, I had simplified my space and time and had begun to live life in flow, and yet, all that was going away, right in front of my eyes as boxes arrived. Each box carried in by one of the five movers brought tears to my eyes, as I saw my simple life of freedom from material things, end. Each box was piled one on top of the other and at the end of the haul, over 500 boxes had entered the house and the villa was uninhabitable.

Thank goodness several good friends from the states had descended on me to help with the moving. They were simply awesome, and the movers had all been efficient and quick - I asked them each to pick something out to take home with them in gratitude for their services. I didn't care what they took - I was not attached to a single thing that had come into the villa. One man took the original Danish dining room chairs covered in zebra skins. Another took a picture of men fishing, one declined to take anything, and one asked if he could have a tablecloth to take to his wife. The last man, the head honcho of the team, asked if he could have a toaster since I apparently had two of them. I gave him the toaster, a blender, and some other appliances. I didn't care and he did, so it was a good deal. I think I would have given away the entire room full of "stuff," in exchange for having my freedom of time and mind back, but that would not happen until I could extricate myself from the Villa two years later.

During those two years my spiritual retreat / bed and breakfast business, ended up being more work than any job I had ever had. The constant upkeep and care of a historic villa 24 hours a day, put the focus of material and money matters constantly in my face. Nothing was simple and solitude was also non-existent.

The day of my closing, I left the new owners with everything inside but my 3 dogs, 2 cats, a bird, and two suitcases. I didn't look back as I headed on my way to a place called simplicity - that place I had learned about in the beginning leg of this journey, and a place which I happily continue to live in, and honor to this day.

"When a man moves away from nature his heart becomes hard."

-LAKOTA SAYING

SACRED LIVING PATH #2

MESSAGE: Savor simplicity.

LESSON: When you slow down, do less and do with less, you will have time to open more and receive the inner riches of balance, peace and freedom

PRACTICES: Stop multi- tasking, let go of acquiring and spend more time indulging in being in nature and taking the time to nurture yourself, you will heal and soften your heart

As I journeyed forward on my path to simplicity, my past experiences of feeling free in simplicity were my motivator. Every time I wanted to buy something, I remembered how I felt with less. It was not worth the sacrifice of my peace-of- mind and freedom of time to 'acquire,' more. Instead, I would enjoy the conscious feeling of being free without it. When I did have to shop, I would go to the animal shelter thrift store first, taking at least one thing to donate, and only purchase things that were under $15. Surprisingly, almost everything I really needed was always there and I got to contribute to a good cause at the same time that I saved money.

Without all of the time spent shopping, cleaning, and accumulating the things that I did not need at all, I had more time to write, paint, meditate, hike, swim, and spend with my dogs walking on the beach. My creative side would open up when I gave myself permission to create instead of consume. I finally had time to write my book.

When I didn't own or have so many things to take care of, I could also keep a simpler routine. On my beach days in my early years on the island, I initially went to the beach with a big bag of stuff to do, but somehow, I would never get to it. When I would pull out a book, phone, or computer to do a chore, I would find myself just putting the project down and just stare back at the sea. My mind would automatically drop into a calm state whenever I was at the beach.

My focus would become singularly focused on whatever was in front of me. Next, I would find myself wanting to go into the water and float, pick up shells, or simply stroll the beach. I went with the flow, and it was so easy. At times, I would chat with people along the way or photograph the clouds. I no longer had an agenda or worried about what I would do next. I soon just brought with me a towel, and visor. Those moments were, and are incredibly freeing and I can always sink quickly into simplicity there.

After every trip to the beach, I would then try to bring this simple routine back home and into work where the chores loom large and duty calls. It didn't come naturally or easily with a strong Puritan work ethic buried in my psyche. The thing that finally worked, was when I made myself stop rushing around and focused on simply doing one thing at a time. I stopped overloading my day with so many "to do's," and simplified my daily list to only a few things each day. With less things to do, I was able to be present and enjoy each activity or project until it naturally concluded. The more I gave myself permission to stay engaged fully with one task at a time, the more it felt like an unfolding, versus a job. What was most surprising was that at the end of the week, everything still got done, but I was so much more relaxed, happy, and free!

"Surrounded by my many things, I'm heavy and weighed down
It took a lot of sweat and tears to gather them around.
My busyness, my need for toys, distract me from the truth
That less is more, and travel light is truly the best route."
-THIA

I am free in simplicity.

*"To offer no resistance to life is to be in
a state of grace, ease and lightness."*
-ECKHART TOLLE

Chapter 3

SINK INTO SURRENDER

Surrender your resistance and control behavior
and dive into the flow of the Universal life
force energy of unlimited potential.
Trust in Divine timing, wisdom and benevolence,
for the Universe is designed to provide
the highest and best for you always.

Surrendering has been a hard thing for me to achieve. Funny that I should put it that way as the path to surrendering is the opposite of achievement. Surrendering, is the path of letting go and releasing expectations, detaching from outcomes, and allowing life to unfold... No resistance please!!

I was an overachiever for the first part of my life. I graduated from high school early, thought it was a waste of time and had three degrees by the time I was 26. My mission was to save all of the disadvantaged people and animals that I could get my hands on. Because my endeavors were altruistic in nature and many unjust things were being done to stray animals and disabled people, I had a tendency to push my agendas, control my circumstances, and resist ineffective outcomes. Feeling justified in this mode as I was fighting for a greater good, I also had lots of strong personal will. Obviously surrender had not found me yet.

What I would eventually come to realize after studying with many wise Eastern teachers was, that there was another way to help and care for others that was actually easy, effortless, and equally effective in achieving the outcomes for others without my ego charging in.

Most Western-minded people think of surrendering as a sign of weakness, that it makes you vulnerable and susceptible to being controlled by others or other circumstances. When the feeling of being controlled is felt, people usually use passive resistance and/or aggressive willfulness to manage their uncomfortable circumstances so that they don't have to feel out of control, which we perceive as making us vulnerable.

We need to understand that becoming vulnerable allows us to surrender our personal will, and thus become open to our Divine Will and access to the field of universal wisdom and love. This is a place of spiritual strength, not weakness. When we surrender our personal will, we get access to the sacred wisdom of Universal Consciousness. You must take the deep dive, and sink fully into the space of total surrender before you get to experience the fruitful flow and benefits of the cosmic river of Divine benevolence and grace.

The path and value to surrendering my personal will was strongly revealed to me during my first Native American ceremony. I had been drawn to study with a Lakota Grandmother whose name was, Grandmother Little Moon. Several of us would go two to three times a week for over a year, to ceremonial sites in deep nature for teachings on sacred ways from Native American life. We would honor our ancestors, Mother Earth, family, and teachers. We would end our ceremonies by sending the sacred smoke of prayers from the peace pipe out to our community and to one another. We had a beautiful community growing, healing and spiritually evolving together from all different walks of life. I eventually lived in this sacred community every day.

I can still remember the first all-night ceremony around the fire. We were to receive teachings on making prayer bundles, or so we thought that was what we were there to learn. We were in an extremely heightened state of spiritual awareness as the sun set that night. We had spent the entire day purifying ourselves with fasting and sweat lodge ceremonies. Our practice was to make 50 prayer bundles and string them all together by morning's light. This may not sound difficult, but while you make the bundle, you are issuing a prayer for the person or situation you are praying for, and the bundles take ten to fifteen minutes to make. I started out priding myself on the efficiency and speed of my bundle making and focusing on my prayers, feeling worried that I had so many people to pray for. After several hours, I could only focus on trying to stay awake, resisting sleep, forcing myself to pray and tie. I got more and more fatigued and frustrated, and pushed to make myself stay awake. Then, I just gave up. My resistance and controlling exhausted me and I stopped thinking about all of it. I wandered through the woods away from the fire and went down to the riverbank. I was just too tired. I sat by the river, listening to it running rapidly, but softly over the rocks. I stilled myself there by the water, and then it happened, I let go of my mind, quietly surrendered and called on the Universe/ Great Spirit to take over.

In the wee hours of the morning, when you are not so easily able to think, focus, or control, surrender often happens naturally. When it does, it allows one to move into the continuum of timelessness and then everything just starts to flow like the river, as if you are in a dream. You become guided by a force from the Universe. You are in flow with it, you move effortlessly through the motions, and your thoughts are almost turned off. My state of surrendering into Divine time seemed to go on for hours, but it was really only two hours that I was in that sweet, sweet sacred space. Nonetheless, bundle after bundle was effortlessly completed while praying.

In the morning, I set my 50 bundles in a basket and went to the table for food without thinking once about what time it was, what was going to happen next, or even where my bundles were going to end up. I felt relaxed, happy, and knew that my prayers had all been heard and answered by The Universe/God/ Great Spirit.

Experiencing the benevolent design and support of the Universe is a huge benefit to surrendering. When you move out of your personal flow and will and into the Cosmic flow of which you are always a part, you receive the clarity and conscious awareness of the synchronicities and support that are all around you all of the time. This awareness can only be seen from that state of surrender.

Some people get to certain states of feeling flow through drugs and alcohol, running, and extreme activity, but unless you enter into Universal flow consciously, you can't sustain it, hence the underpinnings of the cause of the addictive nature in us. We all want to feel the flow all of the time, but only a consciously surrendered ego has access to an unending well of Divine energy.

When we choose to push or resist, vs. letting go and surrendering our personal will, in any moment, we are keeping ourselves out of the flow of the Universal living energies where things are easy and effortless.

Which experience do you want, frustration or flow?

*"Sometimes, when I'm going somewhere, I wait
and then somewhere comes to me!"*
– WINNIE THE POOH

SACRED LIVING PATH #3

MESSAGE: Surrender your personal will to your Divine Will.

LESSONS: Only you are in the way of what you want!

PRACTICES: STOP controlling, pushing, resisting, and START trusting and allowing the benevolent Universal life force energies to flow in and through you full of guidance, synchronicities, opportunity and support.

Now, whenever I sink into that sacred space of surrender, things always begin to happen to help me along, and make it even easier to do whatever it is I am doing. Living in the rhythm and flow of the Universe, instead of pushing, doing, and controlling with my willful mind, I become open to possibilities, new options, synchronicities and solutions that just flow in toward me. When I sink into surrender and go with the flow, I feel lighter, and life almost takes care of itself.

Any time you find yourself in resistance, pushing, controlling, trying to make things happen in your life, and I mean anything, STOP doing it, just STOP! A door is closed for a reason. It's not the right thing, time, person, or place. The first step to surrendering is letting go. Let go of your need to make things happen at that time.

Next, TRUST in the benevolent Universe to provide you with whatever it is you need in the next moment. Then, have the courage to surrender and FREE FALL into the cosmic flow of the Divine river of life force energy surrounding you, where all things are known and understanding exists.

Drink fully from the energies, wisdom, and love from Divine FLOW and RECEIVE all of the benefits and support that you are offered. Feel the flow of the LIGHTNESS of being - it is from this place that you are able to see that surrender is a place of strength and power, not weakness

Whenever I...
Hear myself issuing angry thoughts
Feel my body tight and taught
Keep pursuing fruitless tasks
Want to make another act
And bend to my agenda
I sense I've not surrendered

- THIA

I am light when I surrender.

"People sacrifice the present for the future. But life is available only in the present. That is why we should walk in such a way that every step can bring us to the here and now."
- THICH NHAT HANH

Chapter 4

STAY IN THE PRESENT

Learn to live in each moment in pure
presence so that you can let yourself
be guided by your intuition and
move through life peacefully

Traveling to sacred sites has always been my passion. Places like Stonehenge, Glastonbury, Isle of Sky, Machu Pichu, Lake Titicaca, Giza, Bali, Dharmsala, Sedona, Mt. Shasta, Taos, Varanasi, Delphi and Delos, Mt Kilimanjaro, Palenque and Tulum were my travel destinations in my earlier years.

The sacred nature of the land and the people who live in these spiritually powerful places, is always immediately palpable. People greet one another from their heart and soul essence, fully aware of being a spiritual being having a human experience. On sacred lands, I feel pulsing, high vibrational life force energies moving through me constantly, and I often feel light as a feather. The most significant thing that would happen to me on each of my sacred site journeys was an immediate disconnection from the time space continuum. Only the present moment existed; with the past, and future moments disappearing from my reality.

When I went to live in the African bush to help build schools on a summer college internship, I was initially shocked at the difference in the understanding of time from my Western life. However, it didn't take me very long to get on "Africa time."

In the bush, life was simple because people lived in the moment. During work and food preparation, we would do our jobs without a lot of chitchat among us, just staying very present to our tasks while doing them, and oddly enjoying them more as a result. After work projects were completed, the day always included lots of social time when eating together, and then dancing and drumming around the fire before retiring for the night. The school was being built, but the focus was on being in the moment, sharing life together, enjoying nature, feeling the rhythms of life and honoring and thanking the Creator for the opportunity to do so.

When I visited Machu Picchu, I chose to hike across the Andes for five days into the site. Having flown straight in from the East coast, I was not physically prepared for the altitude effect on my breathing. Two days into the hike, at 15,000 feet, I began to feel so nauseated and out of breath, that I thought that I was going to die. There was no way out and I was having an otherwise amazing experience in the Andes mountains.

We would hike for eight to ten hours a day. As we kept turning around the mountain, the ecology would keep changing. There were magnificent vistas and flora and fauna to feast your eyes on and our group was sharing our thoughts, joys and experiences as we traversed the mountain together. But when each step became more and more laborious, I began to shut down my broad thinking mind. Thoughts of future plans at camp and conversations on our experiences, took a back seat. Instead, I only focused on each moment and each step-in front of me, just to survive. Eventually, this practice became a means to relax me so that I could experience again what was going on outside of me, only without the interference of the problems in my body. I dropped out of my mind and focused on the present moment of my outer experience step-by-step with deep gratitude for being alive active in my heart. I continued like that for two full days, ten hours of hiking a day. Chewing on Cacao leaves, I felt a lessening of the nausea, but the shortness of breath would remain until coming below 12,000 ft. Despite the physical discomfort, living in the NOW had made the two days a memorable, intense, and awesome experience. I remembered almost every image from those 48 hours of single moment experiences.

By the end of the one-week high mountain journey, I was not only feeling relieved to be breathing normally again, but was so anchored into the present moment that it continued with me for the rest of the entire four-week trip. It is said that it takes 90 days of practice to rewire the brain from old behavior patterns, but with minute-by-minute focus on the present moment over the two days, I had amassed thousands of moments, enough to change my brain patterns and behavior. The feeling was as amazing as being in the glorious Andes mountains, with its heart filled people, and powerful Machu Picchu herself. Every experience had become sensorially more acute and real than ever before. I tasted the wind, heard the mountains, and saw colors that were never evident to me before. I felt connected to everything and everyone. Each moment became sacred.

I would re-experience this heightened state of heart-centered sacred awareness in pure presence every time I would travel after that point. When you visit any place and can drop deeply into the present moment, all places and moments become sacred. In that place of pure presence, you become aware of the soul connection to each other and each relationship experience. The earth, when she is engaged and honored in deep presence becomes sacred ceremony, where the Divine exchange takes place. You see yourself as ONE with it ALL. Without the ability to stay in the NOW, you cannot have a sacred journey.

"Doing nothing often leads to the very best of something."
– WINNIE THE POOH

SACRED LIVING PATH #4

MESSAGE: Stay in the present moment of pure presence.

LESSON: Thoughts in the past and future rob us of the NOW moment.

PRACTICES: To drop into and stay in the present moment, stop thinking, talking and rushing; then intuition will take over and inner wisdom will guide you effortlessly and divinely through your day's decisions and dance.

Thoughts are often our nemesis! They are a reflection of our mind's belief system, often full of lack, limitation and concerns. The heart is often full of discomfort and worry from the minds' challenging thoughts. Our mind habitually goes back and forth over the past, and projects those thoughts as possibilities into the future. If you don't believe me, just listen to your mind and write down what you say to yourself for any four to five/ hour period of time. I say... stop thinking over everything, JUST STOP, it's overrated. Turn off your mind and use your intuitive guidance system to navigate instead!

When we let go of our mind, we drop into pure presence and in pure presence, our intuition will naturally take over. Our intuitive guidance system, and we all have it, is innately more intelligent and beneficial for us to use for decision making and direction setting. It is wired directly to our higher mind, heart, and to the Universal field of unlimited knowledge, wisdom and ALL that is. We need only stay open and in the present moment to trust and allow our intuition to activate and operate.

If we stop thinking so much, it is also easier to intentionally stop rushing and multitasking, allowing us to do just one fully-focused thing at a time. Then each experience can happen in a state of pure presence.

Maintaining a single point of focus, is also a great way to get into the present moment. As you engage each task of your daily routine, just focus only on your task; teeth brushing, showering, rinsing dishes, or drinking your coffee as an example. If you begin to get distracted, go outside and walk around and look at the trees or clouds, then come back in and start trying to do this again. If you go to the beach, pick up shells, go into the woods, pick up leaves, go out to the creek, pick up stones. Then you can get in touch with what a single point of focus experience feels like.

Engaging in tasks without rushing and talking, with full focus on each moment of engagement, allows us to break with linear time and have a fuller, more potent and present experience. We sadly believe that to be productive in a Western life, we have to live in a multitasking state most of the time just to get it all "done." This will be a new way of moving through life for many. Try it, you just might like how peaceful it feels!

In the NOW, our experiences will be richer, imbued with intuitive guidance, and sensory adventure not available to us when we are in our endlessly thinking heads or "monkey mind". Also, amazingly, everything will still get done! The goal is to become the moment, swimming in pure presence.

The past and the future contain all the fears
The stories of lack throughout all of the years
Between them, the present, is anchored in bliss
Just try to be blue when you're focused on this
-THIA

I am peaceful in pure presence.

"You were given your gift for the joy you may give in return."
-ELMORE ADDISON

Chapter 5

SHARE YOUR UNIQUE GIFTS

Discover and share your unique gifts
with the world. Learn the importance of
expressing them as service. Serve yourself
and serve others simultaneously.

Ever since I was a little girl, my mother would say that I beat to a different drum. I was always out of sync with my peers, and I didn't care. I wasn't interested in high school social events, but I decorated for the prom and then went home to write a play for my summer neighborhood group. I knew what I liked and didn't like. I had an innate sense of who I was and why I was here, and I was mission- driven all of my life. Because I had a natural sense of self-awareness and confidence, my life path has been filled with adventure after adventure. I've pursued multiple and varied degrees, hobbies and careers in international relations, film-making and photography, performing arts, television, special education, disabilities administration, opera, organizational management, hospitality services, spiritual retreat ownership, animal welfare, energy medicine facilitator, life coaching, motivational speaking, inn managing and mental health counseling. You can do anything that you set your mind to and are passionate about, committed to and are willing to work for!

Throughout my life, whenever I was passionate about, felt inspired to experience, and had some talent in something, I pursued it. When I would engage fully, I would feel alive and empowered and create a fulfilling life for myself and those around me.

Interestingly, when I did what I loved and expressed who I truly was, the money and means were always there to support me. When I occasionally gave up or lost faith that I could create the life I wanted and settled for an inauthentic choice, the money would shrink and so would the opportunities.

We do create our own reality! Change can happen for the better….as soon as we think differently and become authentically aligned. When we are aligned, we are in flow again with Divine life force energies, our life pursuits flow and material ease follows.

Many years ago, I traveled to India to experience life in an Ashram. Most people end up there through spiritual crisis or as part of their yogic training, but I was on a spiritual tour of India that included extensive time in the Ashrams of spiritual teachers. I was at one of my many crossroads in my life, where a work door had closed and the script for the next chapter had not yet been written. This trip became possible as an opportunity to explore more of my inner terrain and excavate my next life path. It was an amazing experience, and through it I began to recognize in myself a deep purpose to become a spiritual teacher.

The days spent in the Ashram, were filled from sunup to sundown with spiritual reflection and personal contemplation as we chanted, read, or listened to talks from the elders. I visited the Ashram of a great avatar, Sai Baba, who many say is an enlightened master. He only made appearances from time-to-time and never spoke, just emanated pure love and light from his being as he walked through the aisles among us.

At one point in a day of prayer, I got separated from my group and was seated with the high elders of the Ashram. At first, I worried about being in the wrong section, but was honored surrounded by their presence. As the day proceeded, I began to notice that they were looking at me as if I was one of them. A young child in the group turned to me on several occasions and kept bowing and saying to me, "Sairam, Sairam, Sairam." I returned the gesture, not realizing that she was acknowledging me as a wise one. Later that evening my spiritual mentor had me reflect on my experience, seeing myself already as a wise one, deeply spiritually devoted in this lifetime. Interestingly, it was not until many years later that I took up this mantle. I had to discover this truth, own it, and live it before I could begin to offer my services as a spiritual life coach, which is my passion and purpose now. Whenever I come into this work, I light up and feel alive. That is how you know that something is your gift to share...

If you are good at it and you love to do it and it helps others!

I have found over the years that if I listened to other's expectations and ideas for me, my life would begin to dwindle and shrink. When we live our life as others see us, or through another, or for another, we begin to lose ourselves and all that we have to offer to the world can get lost. A piece of us dies, our Divine light dims.

For those who are natural caretakers, they easily sacrifice their own time and personal agendas to take care of others in need in their family/friend circle, workplace, often at the complete expense of themselves. I discovered over time that the best way to care-take others and maintain my sense of self and authentic personal agenda, was to embrace the concept of doing life for myself and others "simultaneously". Energy is always being exchanged between people. When we meet our needs while meeting others' needs at the same time, we keep the energy flowing for both parties simultaneously. If energy gets blocked it doesn't flow and without flowing energy in our bodies, we get sick. When we simultaneously engage in giving and receiving with each other we both have energy flowing and stay happy and healthy.

How do we know how to do this? We need to be present in each moment and use our intuitive discernment when interacting with or deciding to choose when and how to interact with others. Using this intuitive process, it provides us with the ability to feel through our intuitive feeling body whether or not, in a moment of decision, choice or action, it is going to serve us both. I will feel relaxed when it is a balanced exchange of energy and I will feel discomfort in my body, confusion in my mind or anxiety in my gut, when it is not a balanced exchange. When I do not honor and take care of myself, I become unbalanced, and if I do too much for others, I unbalance them and myself. Simply put, offering your gifts out into the world in a way that serves you as well as others is a balanced sacred path. I let this be my guidepost for relating now.

Enabling others, doing too much for others continuously, can also keep them from experiencing life challenges that provide the framework for learning their lessons and growing. By taking their own journey of self-discovery and personal transformation away, it might be keeping them from learning about and using their unique talents and gifts that would help make their world and the world a better, happier, and more loving place.

"Compassion is not complete if it does not include oneself."
- ALLAN LOKOS

SACRED LIVING PATH #5

MESSAGE: Share your unique gifts and talents.

LESSON: The world needs each spark of God to flourish.

PRACTICES: Find, shine, and love your unique self! Express yourself while serving others.

Most of us begin to discover our true essence when we are children. We see reflections in all of the people, story characters, and experiences we are naturally attracted to around us. By the age of six, most children are excited to be expressing themselves, as themselves and then, sadly, with school comes judgment. We are discouraged from exploring, and pushing envelopes in any form or manner. Individualization is frowned upon, and fitting in is rewarded. Uniqueness is not valued in the Western school systems and the zest for pursuing one's own personal path and using our imaginations and creative abilities often becomes lost. Most begin to listen to their peers, teachers or parents and plan to do what others approve of. First jobs are often fallen into as a matter of convenience not choice. Life continues on that way and, statistics show that 80% of the people in the western world are not happy in their jobs.

In my spiritual life coaching practice, most of the people I have spoken to, do not feel like they are living their mission or on purpose and most do not feel fulfilled or happy as a result.

All that being said, there is no time like the present to make a change. We have every moment of our life to choose our thoughts, beliefs, and perspectives and when we think and choose differently, life changes accordingly. Once you decide to live authentically and truthfully as YOU, then you're on the path to finding a life of passion and purpose.

If you have problems with the idea of getting in touch with your authentic self, you must embrace the importance of self- love, and recognize that you were put here on this earth to express the unique spark of Creation that you are; that we all are. The Earth was designed to work most effectively when everyone is in the full flow of the expression of their unique talents and gifts, being their authentic self.

To help figure out who you truly are, take a moment and envision yourself going back to your early life, back into your childhood, and remember your fondest moments; those when you felt alive, purposeful, and happy. What were you doing, thinking, feeling? If this is difficult to do, then think over the last week of your life and recall any moments where you were feeling excited, joyful, or serene. What were you doing, thinking, sharing at the time? If you still can't identify your spark, then write down for one week going forward anything that you do that brings you into these feelings. You might be on to something then!

Once you discover your spark, if you feel reluctant to let your light shine out for fear of negative feedback or retribution from others, then put an energy shield around yourself or state an intention, saying out loud, "I am Protected and I am Powerfully living as my Authentic Self ". Then sit in that truth, feeling it fully and wholly believing it and you will be protected. Leave the others to their thoughts and journey and don't spend lots of time talking to, or spending time with anyone who doesn't support you as YOU!

Every day start out acknowledging and appreciating your gifts and talents and let them be the focus of your efforts throughout the day. If your life is not allowing these gifts to be expressed, then you simply need to change your life direction. Take it one step at a time. Create and envision the plan in your mind of what you want to feel and do as your authentic self. Pray on it with desire and call it in from the Universe, staying open and unattached so that you can receive your new life as the highest and best outcome. Remember divine timing.; it may take a while for all things Divine to occur as the Universe always conspires with us to create the most benevolent outcome!

When others' needs come into play that require you to help, support or collaborate with them, consider how to weave their needs and your needs and talents together, using your creative, intuitive capabilities. In this way you write a Divine script for meeting every one's needs simultaneously. When others don't want to keep your needs and agenda in the mix alongside of theirs, then they are possibly not the people or circumstances to engage with for you at this time. It may be another is waiting in the wings to help them, as your gifts are not the ones needed for them in this situation. Or they are not the ones for you to be engaging and collaborating with at this time. We don't need to know how or why. When we follow the intuitive guidance of our inner heart as our authentic self; we will always be serving self and others simultaneously and each person will be empowered and in balance in service out into the world.

"We each are a gift from the heavens above
To share, to sing out our sweet song of love
This is our mission, our purpose, our glee
We make the world better by sharing readily
It's easy to hide or do what they say but
You won't feel alive until you walk your own way"

- THIA

I AM empowered when sharing my unique self.

"Since everything is a reflection of our minds,
everything can be changed by our minds."
- BUDDHA

Chapter 6

SIT IN JOY

Focus your mind on what is
working vs. what is not.
Choose to sit in joy, not pain, and stay in the joy.
Sing your heart's song with gratitude
as often as you can.

The mind is a powerful thing! This is an oft quoted claim but in fact it has been scientifically proven to be true. Thoughts do affect our health, direct our outcomes in the outer world and define the nature of our experiences. Our thoughts powerfully shape and create our life and the world around us. There are Universal Laws that describe the minds role and function in the process of creation and manifestation of our life. My interest in studying the Laws of Attraction and Manifestation, came through my early readings on quantum physics, metaphysical teachings and energy medicine. I was fascinated by the operation of the unseen spiritual energy realms as experienced in my own life, but I was also interested in the science behind it; not to prove it, but to understand it from a functional perspective.

The Laws of Attraction and Manifestation suggest; that as we place our focused thoughts with intention and desire, out into the field of unlimited potential to manifest our reality, the experiences that we attract back to us in return, will be of the same frequency type or nature as that which we send out. Be clear about what you focus on, be aware of the nature of your thoughts and be careful what you ask for.... for you surely will get it. Focus with your mind on positive, high frequency affirming, joyful, loving, sacred thoughts, intentions and desires, and then that will be the nature of what you manifest back.... It is Universal Law that it is so.

The connection between the mind, body and emotions is also very important to understand and master in order to have a healthy and joy filled life. Real life examples of this connection are; when you find yourself in acute pain... and then the dog comes along for a pat, and you give over to the furry hug in appreciation, or a funny commercial comes on and you laugh a lot, or you hear a piece of beautiful music that transports you to another place, a place that is off of the focus of feeling your pain and <u>on</u> the feelings of happiness or joy.... and you begin to relax. You then run 'feel good,' chemistry through your body and it actually stops the physical pain. When we release our negative emotions then we have space to insert positive, appreciative ones. The more positive thoughts and feelings we have, the more we bring healing and healthy change to our body rapidly and completely. Our body is designed to naturally stay healthy and in balance if we feed it positive thoughts, joyful feelings and healthy food as well as live in and move around in nature that is clean and free of toxins.

My first spiritual coaching classes were based around teaching people the importance of and the practice of shifting to higher, more sacred joy-filled thoughts and feelings. Many of my clients were in physical or emotional pain, but my observations often revealed that the deep suffering they were experiencing had to do with a continuous focus on their negative stories, the pain itself, or ineffective situations in their life. There was not much focused attention on positive experiences, feelings of gratitude or joyful thoughts. The goal was to help them learn how to intentionally shift their focus off of pain by intentionally choosing positive, affirming thoughts and feelings instead.

In fact, I practiced this teaching on myself all of the time. Whenever I caught myself engaged in upsetting self-talk, feeling awful and then attracting negative situations, I would stop myself and consciously choose a happier thought or state expressions of gratitude, or conjure more peaceful feelings or circumstances. Within no time, my experience became more uplifted. If I started out intentionally engaging in activities joyfully, being appreciative, and/ or using positive thinking, I had a day full of happy, pain-free experiences... you will receive what you're mind and emotions have conceived.... and believed.

Now belief is the third layer to understand in the Laws of Attraction and Manifestation. Beliefs are so important as, they are the key to permanently resetting your thoughts, emotions and behaviors into more affirming ones. Your beliefs, conscious and unconscious, define the nature of your thoughts, emotions and actions. It is the unconscious component of the mind that you need to be concerned about, excavate and understand. Most assuredly negative, fear-based beliefs are hiding out in your unconscious mind and you want to release them. But in order to do this you must be consciously aware of their existence at some level. Your limited, negative beliefs patterns will look like experiences in your life that feel dense, create poor health and create negative thinking until you take charge and change them. You can reset your buried negative, fear-based beliefs into more sacred, joy affirming patterns just by bringing them into your conscious awareness and choosing to let them go. Once you do actually release them, you will more easily be able to think of and express positive thoughts, feelings and actions throughout your day You will know that you have succeeded when you are in a more upbeat feeling mood and think more affirming thoughts throughout your day.

After returning home from Africa, I was very sick with an intestinal bug that the doctors stateside couldn't cure. I was out of school more then I was in. The very best doctors from Johns Hopkins would tend to me to no avail. My parents were getting very worried. I can still remember the day, sitting outside meditating in my chair by the creek feeling sorry for myself. I started listening and looking at my thoughts and started to see how negative they were and that they were full of doomsday messages. All of a sudden, I began to ask why and to realize that most of my physical malady was rooted in my negative beliefs that coming back into the Western world was going to be awful. I didn't believe that I could have the same Africa experience, sacred and joy filled, deeper, more present anymore; not in my western life. I suddenly recognized that my negative beliefs were the reason why I was holding onto the health problem, as a means to prevent myself from going back into the very non sacred Western world. Next, I surmised that I had a choice; to stay ill, or change my belief about what I believed about this situation. I decided that since I was unable to go back to Africa, I would try to bring the joy of that experience into my current life in the states. I began to think about ways that I could move through my school day and home life more sacredly, with presence, unhurried, and in nature, which I had discovered was important to me on this trip. With a new positive perspective about my current dire situation, I was beginning to have new affirming thoughts and feelings. I started to see a vision as to how I could change how I thought about my day, what I chose to do, how my day would unfold and how I felt about it. I started to believe that I could create the life that I wanted right here and now in Baltimore. I then created that vision where I saw myself returning to Western civilization to live as joyfully as I did in Africa. With a joy filled life again, a sick body was no longer needed or required. The next day I got up and went to school without further discomfort!

A good question to ask yourself whenever you are in physical pain or are suffering emotionally is this; how is this serving me? Honesty is essential for personal growth, spiritual enlightenment, and the maintenance of good physical health. You need to get to the root cause of your pain and suffering, by courageously and willingly exploring your victim belief patterns surrounding your illness. The accompanying negative thoughts and emotions and often the physical health malady itself offer clues and information as to what it may be. What is most often revealed in victim-hood belief excavation is a sense that you do not have any control over changing your situation to realize a more positive outcome. But remember… the mind is a powerful thing!

Another great example in my own life of the positive power of the mind, took place on a train trip through Northern India. I was on the way to visit the Dali Lama's residence and meet his teachers in Dharamshala. It was one of the years that India and Pakistan were at war and for the entire train journey, we heard bombs and jets flying overhead. Fear and anxiety were already in the air, never a good friend of healing. Unfortunately, after the first night in our rail cars, many had acquired a rash of bed bug bites, small and irritating for some, but for me it was intense. I'm allergic to bug bites and hundreds of bite welts covered my entire body. Not only was it intensely itchy, it was painful to think that I would be unable to fully experience my time with the teachers in the Himalayan Mountains. I decided to go to bed that night filled with the belief that I was going to be healed and with the conviction to focus my thoughts on the excitement and the joy of my travel destination and on the positive effects that the medicine they had given me, was going to have on me. I awoke surprisingly to almost no rash the next day. This was not a typical result for the medicine to work so quickly. In fact, it was next to miraculous. I was in such gratitude the rest of the ride. I was also keenly aware that I had co-created that positive outcome with my thoughts.

Concurrently, I observed that, those people on the train who stayed mentally negatively focused on their discomfort, they continued to have rashes accompanied by intense physical suffering for many days ahead. Interestingly though, once we arrived at the Monastery everyone became well; all of our thoughts, feelings and focus was at a higher vibrational level; peace, gratitude, love and joy frequencies, where suffering does not exist. Coincidentally, these were the Dharma teachings we would be engaged with while in the monasteries. Focus on pain, stay attached to it and we get more of it - it's called suffering! Detach from the pain-filled thoughts and feelings in our minds and heart and focus on bliss, peace, and gratitude and we get more of it - it is called Nirvana!

"When you do things from your soul you feel a river moving in you, a joy"
- RUMI

SACRED LIVING PATH #6

MESSAGE: Sit in joy more often.

LESSON: Whatever we choose to focus on we get more of. Choose to find and focus from your heart on joy and sit and stay there as often and long as you can

PRACTICES: Detach from suffering by not focusing on pain and unhappiness, instead move toward what brings you JOY. Start by being grateful for all that is working in your life.

How do you discover what brings you joy?! Ask yourself what things, experiences, events, people, thoughts and places make you smile, make your heart sing, make you relaxed, excited, and feel alive! We often know what they are, but don't feel like we can engage them too often or we will not be acting responsibly or practically. The Puritan work ethic is ingrained in Westerners' minds, often dictating the need to do multiple mundane chores and manage all responsibilities before you can have fun. My advice is to look at every day as if it were your last, with death on your shoulder, like the Shamans teach us. Not with fear but with awareness of the availability of choice to define the nature and the quality of your days experience. What would you choose to do, to say, to feel and who would you be with if this day were to be your last day on Earth? In fact, none of us know if that might not be the realty of our next day. I don't know about you, but I want to spend my last day, and really every day, being in the energy of joy as often as possible! This is truly a high vibrational sacred path!

Some suggestions for creating a path to JOY would be; to make your daily To Do list comprised of all of the joy filled experiences you love and want to integrate into your life every day. Imagine actually doing this for one week. Take all of those purely joy filled activities and put them at the top of your daily To Do list.

You can envision all of your required day-to-day tasks or chores and re-frame them; reflecting a more alive, fun filled version. Take the most serious of your responsibilities and find a way to infuse a delightful moment in it for yourself, and everyone involved in it with you. This is a great exercise for bringing joy to the front and center of your life, every day. Also, in pure presence joyful experiences are amplified.

So, STAY in the JOY; STAY there and bathe in it. We spend far too much time lingering in our moments of pain, discomfort, anger and suffering and hardly spend any time in our joyful ones. Change the time/energy quotient. You build your light body that way and eventually start to become the energy of joy; radiating and offering this high vibrational frequency out to the world.

"When you rise in the morning, give thanks for the light, for your life,
for your strength. Give thanks for your food and for the joy of living-
if you see no reason to give thanks, the fault lies in yourself"
- TECUMSCH (LEADER OF THE SHAWNEE)

Another way to raise your frequency into joy is through issuing gratitude for all that is working in your life and all that you do have. Send appreciation to all those who have helped to support you on your life path. Offer a gift to Mother Earth for all of her abundant life sustaining gifts. I place offerings of flowers and seashells under my oak trees each morning in gratitude for the bounty that Mother Earth provides me with every day. This is sacred reciprocity or Ayni, as taught and practiced by the Q'ero medicine men and women of Peru… whenever you take or receive anything, you give something back to keep the energy in balanced flow, both personally and planetarily.

There are always things to be grateful for when you put your mind to it. Thank Mother Earth for her beautiful healing playground, Thank the air for cooling you and the sun for warmth, the trees for oxygen and the waters for hydrating you. Thank the soil for its nourishment and the flowers for their beauty. Be grateful for the bees that pollinate so that we have food to eat. Thank the workers who grow your food and those that deliver it. Bless your Mother and Father for giving you birth and for the Source/ God/Great Spirit for giving you Life and also for creating such a Divine and benevolent Earth home. There is so much to be grateful for that naturally surrounds you every day. This exercise will always raise your energy frequency and make you feel better if you are down. And remember, whatever you focus your attention on you get more of…so more attention on appreciation and gratitude, more appreciation will come your way. From the seeds of appreciation and gratitude grows a joy filled life.

> *"What will you choose, the option is yours*
> *Do you want pain or sadness or chores?*
> *If joy is your counsel, your guide and your star*
> *Then sit in this moment that's rightfully yours*
> *Remember to hold on, when joy hits the scene*
> *And savor and bathe in it never to leave"*
>
> **- THIA**

I AM joyful when focused there.

*"When we recognize the virtues, the talent, the beauty of Mother Earth,
something is born in us, some kind of connection, LOVE is born."*
- THICH NHAT HAHN

Chapter 7

SOURCE LOVE FROM THE SOURCE

You will always experience unconditional love
when you are divinely connected to the Creator,
nature, and the cosmos. They are always
there for you to experience all of the time.
Receive the constant blessings from the field
of unlimited potential, omnipresent wisdom
and infinite love, as is divinely designed,
to be available to us all of the time.

I went on a six-month hiatus after closing my spiritual retreat center. It had been a wonderful, but draining 24/7 experience. Before I even started on this journey, I had been an over-giver, caretaker type, on my way to major personal health issues. Clearly, on the backside of it all, I realized that I was the one who had needed the retreat experience and had not allowed myself to receive healing when it was needed most. I had to take time off and put my focus on healing my body which was chronically fatigued and failing. I was given the opportunity to stay in a beautiful cottage overlooking the Caribbean Sea on a 2000- acre cattle ranch. I was all by myself, except for my dogs and the abundance of nature all around me. I locked the gate and didn't reappear for four months.

During that time, I dove into a myriad of books and opened my mind as wide as I could to all of the healing tools available in all of the traditions. Intermittently, I began to practice just being; being with nature, being with the Creator, being with the cosmos. I would lie in my hammock outside for hours and spend my entire day and night consciously BEING. A month into my retreat, I began to literally see the Universe at work. It was nothing short of miraculous. I saw cause and effect from my every thought and action. When I requested anything, an answer, an insight, an opportunity, a new teaching, it would show up in some way if not immediately, then soon thereafter.

Once I started going slowly back out into the outer world, I would be thinking about a friend and the phone would ring and it would be that friend who I'd been thinking of. I wanted to meet with my landlord about getting a screen door and he came up to visit saying that he had been thinking about putting up a screen door! I wanted to find a specific healing herb and someone in line at the market came up to me spontaneously and told me where to go for it. In the herb shop they were doing a workshop on my recent reading material. It just kept happening like this.

Because I had seen that the Universe was designed to respond to all of my heartfelt requests, and now I believed this to be so, whenever I sent an intention out into the Universe, I asked, listened and looked for a response, the blessings appeared. The Source created Universe was designed to gift us whatever we asked for from our hearts every minute of every day! I was experiencing the Infinite all- knowing Universe as Unlimited Potential.

In the Shamanic and Indigenous worlds, one always feels and sees the truth of our infinite nature, the divineness of all beings, the sacredness of life itself, our connection to each other, to all of life, to the cosmos, and our Creator/ Source/God. It is understood that, all that is seen and unseen in the Universe, and that includes us, is comprised of unlimited living energy, constructed of infinite Divine LOVE, Creative Potential and Aware Consciousness.

In the Western world most people do not see or believe in this reality. Most see with limited human sight only. With lack and limitation all around them, people in fear, pain and suffering, separation and survival thinking it is easy to believe that this version of life is the only reality. People say, "how does a loving Creator allow this", not realizing that it is the human with limited beliefs who has created the current limited earth reality. When humans manifest from lower frequency belief patterns, they no longer: know themselves as spiritual beings or see the existence of Source or feel their connection to Nature. Sacred higher wisdom, knowledge of the truths of the unlimited loving nature of the

Universe, Planet Earth and humanity becomes "veiled ", until humans undergo a spiritual awakening (unveiling) process.

The choice to take the journey of spiritual awakening is always available to every human all of the time. But in Western societies, where people are so attached, enamored and distracted by their material reality, they don't often choose that journey proactively. They wait instead until they become sick, are abused, abandoned, in loss or pain. Fortunately, the way you arrive to the start your journey to spiritual awakening and LOVE doesn't matter. Whenever one is ready to take a vertical climb it is time. The hope is that you get on the journey sooner than later so that you can begin to experience the unconditional love that you are and that is available to you all of the time on spirit time.

There are many different paths to take to awaken to spiritual reality. Most of them teach one how to connect directly to Divine Source energy where wholeness and holiness already exist. There are many Dharmas and doctrines from formal religions, sacred cultures and faiths, that provide paths to this end; paths that lead to living as deep peace and pure love through connection with a higher source. Teachers have come from all traditions throughout time to wake up those who have fallen under the veil. Their message has almost always been the same at the core of their teachings. They have always come to remind people of the TRUTH of their higher Universal infinite self and of the reality and existence of an infinitely loving Universe, Creator/ God/Source of all that is, of which they are at One with. When we reach this state of remembering ourselves as infinite and connected to everything, we experience DIVINE Source LOVE all of the time. When we are living as infinite and unlimited spiritual beings having a human experience, then we are there, sacredly in LOVE, as Source LOVE itself.

Deeply connecting and communicating with Nature offers a spiritual awakening path to Source LOVE. Encoded in nature is the total Divine reality of the Universe. Through deep nature experiences we can come to see the infinite Universal energies that exist everywhere around us all of the time My own way of spiritually connecting and filling myself up, is to spend time in nature every day, in appreciation, prayer, joy, and presence. When I walk amidst nature, I connect to the Universal life force in each plant, tree, animal, bug, and moreover, all Divine creations. When I sit in nature and contemplate and commune, I get a joyful and love filled feeling from the deepness and vastness of this relationship. Then from a deep place of appreciation in my heart, I give thanks, give an offering, ask for forgiveness and send love, and honor to the entire Earth Kingdom, Cosmos, and the Source of Creation, for their gifts to me and all of humanity. In the end I merge and become one with ALL.

If I can kayak on the water at sunset or walk out on the beach, I'll work my day around it. A healing and spiritual connection takes place with Mother Earth and the Creator at every sunset experience, at every shell collecting beach walk, every swim in the sea, every hike in the woods, or hammock time out under my live oak trees. If I begin my day in meditation and ceremony at the park with my dogs, I start out feeling filled with peace and in balance heading into the world of human neediness, financial challenges, and global pain. Then when I step into my days tasks, my daily experiences are colored brighter and lighter feeling more love as a result. I then can more easily use each subsequent moment as an opportunity to infuse and maintain more of my Divine connection as I move through the rest of my day with my fellow human travelers.

Walking in nature is one way to spiritually connect to Creator, see the God in all things, and align with your higher-self. There are also many other practices to this end; if praying, chanting, meditating, reading spiritual teachings, singing, qigong, yoga, dancing, drumming, hiking, biking, sailing or anything else you can do in nature assists you to connect up spiritually, then follow that path and make it part of your daily life every day! Each of us need to find and forge our own way to this sacred destination.

It's also essential to be able to receive the blessings on this path once connected. Our patterns of 'less than,' not deserving, and other distractions, can keep us from seeing and receiving the healing gifts of LOVE and opportunities the Source and Universe showers on us every minute of every day. We must consciously choose to see ourselves as worthy and as we get connected, aligned and resonating with Source energy, we will have so much more ability to love ourselves and others more fully and unconditionally.

"...,.for this is the message that you have heard from the beginning, that we should love one another."
-JESUS OF NAZARETH

SACRED LIVING PATH #7

MESSAGE: Source unconditional LOVE from the SOURCE of Creation and share this LOVE with others.

LESSON: Humans cannot fill their need for unconditional LOVE with each other but should turn to Source Creator/ God/ Great Spirit which is Divine unconditional LOVE, and when you merge with Source you become that LOVE that is all around you and is you, as the matrix of everything.

PRACTICES: Connect to Source Energy/God/Creator directly or when in nature or at sacred places throughout the day to increase your awareness of yourself as Divine energy and unconditional love and then share that LOVE with others.

What is your current spiritual practice? Anchor in one that is already serving you, but do it every day or even twice a day. Explore a new option for spiritual inspiration and engagement mentioned in this chapter. Just ask the Universe to send you the answers and it will appear right in front of you. The Universe always has your back and your best interest at heart!

If you do not have a current spiritual affiliation or practice, then explore the great spiritual traditions on our planet that offer diverse ways to connect with your spiritual-self. Visit a Monastery, Ashram, Cathedral, Temple, Church, Sweat Lodge, Mosque, Synagogue or Chapel and begin to feel the Divine essence of the sacred space connect in you. Meditate, contemplate, and go deeply within asking for guidance and listening for direction. Sit for however long it takes to connect in, receiving a Divine message or feeling. Ultimately, open to your own Divine essence and feel it fully; merging with Source LOVE energy as you.

Plan to spend time in nature every day in some way, shape, or form. Eventually just "being," there for periods of time connects you directly to Divine energy. Nature holds the highest vibration on the planet. It is amazing, spiritual perfection, and a healing tool as well, available immediately to anyone, anytime. In inclement weather times, bring nature inside with flowers, plants, and pets to carry on the healing vibe. Spend time interfacing with all the other sentient beings we tend to overlook. Show them love and gratitude for their service to the planet and its people. Without our nature friends, we will not survive. Protect the environment and local ecologies that you inhabit. Reduce your footprint on the Earth by consciously consuming sustainably, humanely, and naturally. Be a good steward of the Earth and she will return the blessings ten-fold in the form of healing and well-being, every time you turn to her. As you honor and thank all beings, your understanding of true interconnection will grow.

The journey is taxing when going alone
We each want some friendship at work or at home
Support feels like tonic, we can't get enough
But each person's journey makes their well leak a lot
For humans are limited so they can't give enough
To fill up our wells with unlimited love
It's found in Creation, in Nature and Source
We need to drink deeply of that vertical course
Reminding ourselves to play well with each other
But make no mistake our best source is The Mother

- THIA

I AM loved when sourced by the Source

When you walk the SEVEN PATHS to SACRED LIVING and become serene in solitude, simply engaged, surrendered to intuition, staying present to everything, share your purpose, sustain joy, source love through your connection to Source and Nature; you remember your blessed, reverent and holy spirit self.... and in that moment, you are there, sacredly living and your life becomes a walking prayer!

THE 7 SACRED PATHS

Messages	Lessons	Practices
1) Seeking Solitude is necessary	Too much "Doing," is a distraction and keeps us from getting into relationship with our inner selves	Be still, listen deeply, get grounded Release your victim self, see objectively
2) Savor simplicity	When you do less and do with less you get more of what you really need	Stop multitasking and rushing, let life unfold Let go of stuff, spend time w/ inner riches
3) Sink into Surrender	Only you are in the way of what you want	Stop controlling, pushing, resisting Trust in Divine Will, Timing, and Benevolence
4) Stay in the present	Thoughts in the past and future rob us of the NOW moments	Stop thinking, let intuition guide you Stay present, mindful and feel pure presence
5) Share your gifts	The world needs your spark of God Source to flourish	Find, love, express and shine your unique you Serve self along with others
6) Sit in joy more	Whatever we focus on is what we get more of	Move toward what makes your heart sing Be grateful for all that is working in your life
7) Source your LOVE from Source/Creator/God	Conditional humans cannot provide unconditional LOVE to each other; do not expect it	Connect to Source LOVE through Nature to receive inspiration and blessings and be that LOVE to each other

PRACTICE INSTRUCTIONS

Each of the 7 sacred paths has a key component for living a sacred life every day. They do naturally build on each other, however, there is no order to spiritual growth, self-care, and personal development. You can start with the first path or begin with the practices in the chapter that most resonate with you, or are illuminating an area of your life needing support or change. Go down a path for at least one month, or until you begin to experience a shift toward a more sacred experience within your day-to-day life in that area. If you take on each of the seven paths over the course of a year, your daily life will definitely become much more sacredly alive!

GOING DEEPER...

If you need or want to go deeper into developing practices and ways to live more sacredly, then you can continue on to the sacred healing journeys illustrated in the workbook in Section II.

This section will provide you with prescribed sacred healing and rejuvenation practices that support living sacredly everyday.

By engaging in spiritual self-inquiry, using natures' healing energies, you can more easily recognize and release your blocks and stress and reset your field Divinely, going from being a restricted to an expansive YOU!

Remember, whatever we choose to focus on, we get more of....

SECTION II

A Call to Sacred Living - The Workbook

Individual Healing Journeys
For The Sacred Traveler

7 Sacred Healing Journeys to help you learn to...

- **U**ncover limited blocks and beliefs causing stress
- **R**elease victim patterns and get clarity of purpose
- **N**avigate raising your vibration into joy, peace, and love
- **E**xpand and live in balance, health and harmony

FIND THE JOY IN THE **JO**-U-R-N-E-**Y**

SEVEN PATHS FOR SACRED LIVING

I have put the Seven Sacred Paths into Seven Sacred Healing Journeys that include experiential practices that you can do every day to help you release the blocks and beliefs of lack, limitation and emotions of fear within you; opening your life to more peace, health and joy. As you reset your patterns of distortion into divine ones, you raise your personal vibration into the power, wonder and adventure of sacred living.

FIND THE JOY IN THE **JO**-U-R-N-E-**Y**
Once you compassionately U-uncover, and R-release,
from your old limited way of life, and spiritually N-navigate
and E-expand, you can en**JOY** a more sacred one!

Life is a continuous journey of choices, decisions, feelings, desiring, actions and pauses. We experience it all through a lens of our own creation. The one thing ALWAYS in our control is our lens, our choice of perspective. We can, most simply put, come from the lens of Human fear and stress and only see in a separated and limited way, producing limited resulting experiences in our life or, we can see through the Sacred lens of unity, unlimited love and potential, which will produce limitless experiences of joy and bliss. The choice is a simple one in each moment, but the human mind is rather complex and full of many limited beliefs that require rewiring in order to see through Divine eyes again. How do we do this you might ask?

One way to do this is to <u>practice</u> seeing and doing life through a sacred lens. By facilitating deeper spiritual connection through daily time spent prescriptively in Nature, a sacred lens is created to support your own healing. Through a sacred lens you can then uncover limiting blocks and beliefs to release and discover unlimited ones to adopt. You will then navigate your daily life from restrictive living into a more expansive way. The Seven Sacred Healing Journeys with practices contained in this workbook section, are a guide to that end!

Practices <u>are</u> necessary because of the difficulty inherent in humans' relationship to making change. The difficulty starts with the mind. Let's look at how our mind is designed. It is wired first for survival and change is perceived as a threat to safety and survival. The mind does <u>not</u> want change.

Our mind directs thoughts that are constructed of our belief system. The subconscious mind is comprised of belief imprints from the lower and higher versions of our own, our parent's, our culture's and our society's beliefs. Some are trauma belief imprints from experiences that caused fear which made us feel like we were going to be neglected, abandoned, harmed or die. These fear-based beliefs are often buried by the mind and suppressed, so that we won't revisit them as another uncomfortable or painful experience, as a protection mechanism from this. This is why we are designed to resist change!

The body and mind hold onto these trauma experiences throughout our life, and we all have them, until we consciously choose to let them go. We don't let them go easily, because the feelings of discomfort and pain that arise when we start to think about or talk about them is uncomfortable. In the process of release we tend to further ignore/bury, instead of move through the emotions of fear, feeling them fully and then releasing them. The root cause of most pain, suffering, and disease is the holding on to these trauma stories, fear emotions, limited beliefs and fight or flight behaviors as a way of avoiding discomfort.

> *"Efforts to manage our pain, not to feel it, are the basic cause of illness.... rooted in our childhood traumas"*
> **- DR. GABOR MATE (TRAUMA SPECIALIST)**

Trauma experiences can also make us feel like we have been separated from Love/God, and can turn our all-knowing authentic spiritual mind, trusting in and believing that we are connected to and actually are unconditional Source love and wisdom, into one without these spiritually empowering beliefs. When the spiritual Source connection becomes lost, Divine LOVE is questioned. When we begin to believe that the world is not unconditionally loving, love appears to be limited, we lose hope, strength, resilience, and comfort. Redefining our spiritual perspective is hard as we are now unconsciously holding onto this distortion pattern to avoid pain and discomfort that comes with the necessary inner process involved in changing our beliefs. We feel like change is too hard and that we cannot make changes possibly at all or at the very least, easily.

The good news is that, you can teach an old dog new tricks as well as a new dog new tricks! Our brain is retrainable, neuroplastic which means that <u>through repeated practice of setting new intentions,</u> we rewire and strengthen positive neural pathways and that similarly, we weaken other negative pathways when we let them fall into disuse. Our DNA is not fixed either, it is simply an imprint of our changing belief patterns and our biology follows suit. Thank you, Dr. Bruce Lipton and others, for this cutting edge new medical information.

All of our fear based subconscious beliefs and survival patterns <u>can</u> be changed, rewired and released gracefully by engaging in sacred living practices from Section I which raise your perspective out of survival into a more observer, objective view so that you are able to release those fear emotions of the victim in a safe, calm and non-judgmental way. When we courageously choose to uncover and change our limited, restrictive fear-based beliefs and behaviors formed from life's traumas; (fears and feelings of being abandoned, not being good enough, not being safe, not being deserving), the <u>choice itself to change</u> allows our mind to begin to release us from survival thinking. Then we create the space within ourselves for new unlimited spiritual thoughts to arise. When we then practice choosing to consciously cultivate and navigate our way back to a more spiritually expanded and unlimited set of Divine beliefs, thoughts, emotions and behaviors; (I am a divine creation, I am infinite, I am loved, I create my own reality, I am gifted), with continued engagement, we strengthen those Divine beliefs within ourselves. We will have gone into deep personal self inquiry and will have ultimately cultivated within us a powerful <u>sacred personal lens</u> for upliftment and empowerment to start to create a more Divine life. We are stepping into Divine power!

We have thousands of moments every day to engage in these sacred personal change practices that support Divine beliefs and behaviors, allowing us to more easily release our dysfunctional survival behaviors and trauma imprints and emotions. These practices that support the creation of new, more sacred ways of thinking, feeling and "seeing" will also positively change our lives, our health, and our relationship to the world.

The final change tool in the tool kit is our choice of setting in which sacred personal change transpires. In nature we have a natural healing environment. When we become imbued with Natures spiritual energy, it elevates us to a place of higher sight and wisdom, gaining greater insights and better direction for making change. If we allow the painful emotions and experiences to be expressed in the loving and healing arms of Mother Earth, then we can much more easily shift our belief patterns and emotions from limited, to LOVE again. Our healing opportunities in nature are available to us all of the time, every minute of every day.

Mother Nature will provide the stage and support for most of the sacred healing journeys illustrated in this workbook. The Nature Kingdom is a Divine creation as is the human body and we have it at our disposal all of the time, for healing, inspiration, nurturing, guidance and play. Nature, Source and spiritual human...what Divine power this union can unleash!

"The indescribable innocence and beneficence of Nature---
of sun and wind and rain, of summer and winter,---
such health, such cheer, they afford forever!!"

"Shall I not have intelligence with the earth? Am I not
partly leaves and vegetable mould myself?"
-HENRY DAVID THOREAU

LIFE IS A JOURNEY AND EVERYTHING IS SACRED

The practices in each of the following healing journeys will help you let go of 7 limited beliefs that we all share in modern society, and replace them with seven sacred beliefs and behaviors. They contain sacred practices cultivated and combined from ancient wisdom teachings, metaphysical laws, and modern science. These practices can be put into play in your everyday life. You can do them even with responsibilities at home, with a family, or while in a challenging job. Take an area of your life that feels most restricted, limited, or in need of change; an area where there is lack, ineffectiveness, discomfort, pain, problems or disease setting in. Start there and make a commitment with the intent, and your heart's desire to become happier and healthier in that particular area of your life!

Become a sacred traveler; heal, expand, & live in joy!

THE SEVEN
SACRED HEALING JOURNEYS

From RESTRICTION ⟶ EXPANSION

SEEK SOLITUDE and go from BUSY ⟶ STILLNESS
"I AM CLEAR"

SAVOR SIMPLICITY and go from COMPLEXITY ⟶ EASE
"I AM FREE"

SINK INTO SURRENDER and go from RESISTANCE ⟶ FLOW
"I AM LIGHT"

STAY PRESENT and go from WORRY ⟶ WONDER
"I AM PEACEFUL"

SHARE YOUR GIFTS and go from CONTRIVED ⟶ ALIVE
"I AM EMPOWERED"

SIT IN JOY and go from MUNDANE ⟶ MAGICAL
"I AM GRATEFUL"

SOURCE LOVE FROM SOURCE and go from LIMITED ⟶ INFINITE
"I AM LOVE"

Sacred Preparation

Before you enter into any one of your sacred healing journeys, sit still and close your eyes for the first ten to fifteen minutes and breathe in the light from the Creator into your head and down through your body envisioning a pillar of light around you, embracing you in source love.

On the next breath release any negativity from your day and send this into the Mother Earth grounding yourself into the core of the Earth and issue gratitude for this support from the Mother.

With another breath bring in that love energy from Mother Earth back up into your body and let it reside in your heart, relaxing and calming you as you breathe in and out. Hug yourself and allow the divine Mother and Father love energies emerge in your heart.

Then, on another breath send it out as love from your heart, out to the world around you and expand into your cosmic self, remembering that you are a Divine being, connected to everything and everyone, and that everything is sacred.

Do this for several minutes until you feel a state of calmness and serenity.

Now you are ready to begin your engagement with any sacred healing journey that you desire to go on.

Seek Solitude

SACRED HEALING JOURNEY #1
On the path from BUSY ⟶ STILLNESS "I AM CLEAR"

Seek solitude, this is the first sacred journey for a reason; when we are engaged with others/things we can't be alone. Without time alone, we cannot be still and if we are not still, then we cannot be silent to hear sacredly. We often do anything we can to avoid being alone by ourselves. Engaging in distractions from self is almost seen as a noble endeavor and is addictive in modern culture. When we maintain constant busyness and interaction with our outer world, through social media, communications, material acquisitions, and obligations, the mental material mind reigns and we have no ability to listen to the still Divine voice within. This hinders us from understanding who we really are, and what we are really here to do with our lives, which is to live life in joy and to manifest our dreams of service into existence. We need alone time to gain perspective on our inner world and to ideally cultivate our observer, nonreactive, sacred lens. It is crucial if one wants to lead an effective sacred life, that we commit time spent in solitude, every day, to that end. In that place we call solitude, all the truths are revealed.

STILLNESS PRACTICE

The first step is to find that special "solitude" spot, in your house, outside your home, or on your drive home, ideally outdoors always if possible. Make sure that it is a place that you can go to daily. You will be working with the healing element of water, and engaging in a healing release water meditation. We often distract ourselves from being alone because we do not want to experience the emotional discomfort that can arise from thinking about negative past or future, painful and/or ineffective experiences when we are all alone. We must release the fear of this potential experience and allow the feelings of emotional discomfort to arise and be released by courageously taking the first step in committing to spending time alone.

In this practice, you'll be going into solitude but with the conscious awareness that as discomfort arises, by being engaged in a sacred healing space, you will go to the other side of that discomfort. Go into your alone space/place and begin by sitting down and getting still. Close your eyes and do the 10-15 minute sacred preparation exercise (on page 49) to bring in light from the Universe to release you from your day, ground you in the love from Mother Earth and then use it to heal your heart and expand you by sending it back out through your heart. This is sacred preparation for any sacred journey.

Start a beach meditation. At the beach, life is always serene and relaxed.

Keep your eyes closed and envision yourself all alone on a deserted beach, sitting down on the sand by the water's edge.

Feel the waves begin to slowly come up and lap around your legs as you sit on the sand, wave after wave relaxing you as it washes gently around your feet and legs but never washes over you.

Listen, just sit and listen to the waves, do this for a while. As the victim stories come up and through you at first, just listen to these stories of what is not working or right in your world; that which makes you unhappy or uncomfortable. As they arise, let the waves wash over you and carry out the negative thoughts or experiences you hear. Let the water take them and begin to consciously cleanse all that is unhappy, all that is negative, all that is hurtful, all that is stressful in your life. Do not hold on to these feelings or judge them. Just watch them, feel them and let them go!

With each wave of water, intend to cleanse, cleanse, cleanse...release, release, release these negative experiences and feelings of lack until you feel a sense of emptiness. Do this for as long as it takes to feel empty, and then breathe softly until you leave your busy self behind and come into a state of stillness.

Spend another five minutes breathing softly and slowly, consciously breathing in health and happiness to fill in that space that you're cleansing and clearing has left; breathing out any mental negativity, emotional pain, and any physical discomfort that is still left, and breathing in health, harmony, and happiness.

End your meditation fully focused in stillness on new, affirming visions and desires as or if they arise. If only emptying occurs, partial or full, let that be your experience for that session. Using the element of water, you release, heal, and gain power in the serene stillness where clarity begins to arise knowing that all will be well.

"...the mere sight and sound of water can induce a flood of neurochemicals that promote wellness, increase blood flow to the brain and heart and induce relaxation. Thanks to science, we're now able to connect the dots to the full range of emotional benefits being on, in, or near the water can bring.... And contact with water induces a meditative state that makes us happier, healthier, calmer, more creative, and more capable of awe."
(AN EXCERPT FROM "BLUE MIND" BY WALLACE NICHOLS)

Repeat this beach meditation using the element of water at least three to four times a week. As you clearly envision the water, it will be as if the water is really washing over you for your body's healing. Our minds imaginal capacity will trigger our body actions, just by envisioning the actions, the same as it will in actual action. If you can go to a water source do that! You'll soon begin to experience a feeling of serenity after each meditation. Each time, give yourself the time to release your negative beliefs, and begin to see the truths of its effect on your health and happiness. As the visions of the new, clearer picture of your desired beliefs and life is revealed, use your journal in this workbook and write down the information shown.

See yourself as a positive conscious creator in charge of creating a positive life for yourself with new beliefs. Allow the water to help you take away your pain and negativity every day and eventually, by spending time in stillness, you will be able to hear your empowered, authentic-self and begin to see the life you want to create and live. State to yourself until you are feeling the truth of it..." When I seek solitude, without busyness, in stillness I am clear and serene."

JOURNEY #1

COMMENTS and CONCLUSIONS

After every sacred solitude session, as often as you can, journal and record your experience. Record a response, thought, feeling, problem, or achievement. Use words, pictures, note, or poetry to make your points, and look at them at least once a week to see what your reflective-self has to say about these comments. Make another journal entry on the reflections of your writings weekly in addition to your daily journey activity experience notes. As you go deeper into looking and feeling your way through your release and reset journey new levels of insights will constantly be revealed until you get to the root of it all.

This is a journey ultimately of self- discovery using your own process and perspectives on the path to sacred living to help develop your sacred-self. At the end of a month, draw themes of limited beliefs and patterns that you want to continue to consciously release as they arise. Themes of the new sacred beliefs that you want to embrace are beginning to become apparent as you use the element of water to cleanse, release, and clarify your life during your sacred solitude time.

MONTH I_____
Describe your experience on each date:

Date:

Date:

Date:

Date:

Date:

Date:

Date:

Date:

Date:

Date:

MONTHLY NOTES:

MONTHLY THEMES:

Limited Patterns to Release   Sacred Patterns to Reset

MONTH 2_____

Describe your experience on each date:

Date:

Date:

Date:

Date:

Date:

Date:

Date:

Date:

Date:

Date:

MONTHLY NOTES:

MONTHLY THEMES:

Limited Patterns to Release   Sacred Patterns to Reset

MONTH 3_____

Describe your experience on each date:

Date:

Date:

Date:

Date:

Date:

Date:

Date:

Date:

MONTHLY NOTES:

MONTHLY THEMES:

Limited Patterns to Release   Sacred Patterns to Reset

CONCLUSIONS:

I release the following limited beliefs

I reset to the following sacred beliefs

MY STILLNESS MANTRA

WHEN MY OLD LIMITING BELIEFS ARISE, I OBSERVE THEM WITHOUT JUDGMENT, FEEL THE FEELINGS THAT ARISE WITH THEM FULLY AND THEN LET THE FEELINGS AND BELIEFS GO.

WITH MY NEW AWAKENED AWARENESS, IN STILLNESS, I REFOCUS MY INTENTIONS ON MY SACRED BELIEFS AND DESIRES AND KNOW IT TO BE SO!

Savor Simplicity

SACRED HEALING JOURNEY #2

On the path from COMPLEXITY ⟶ EASE "I AM FREE"

Do we live modern life in complexity because we think we have to? There is a wonderful story of an old fisherman who takes a wealthy man out on his boat for a vacation day. The wealthy man states that his dream is to retire so that he doesn't need to do anything but fish all day like the boatman. He goes on to tell the boatman about all of the money and material things that he has, all of the important things that he does, how tired he often is, and sometimes, how irritable and sick from it all he is, but that he feels better when he dreams of the day he is just fishing every day. The simple boatman keeps looking at him oddly the more he speaks of his life, until he bursts out laughing and suggests that he needn't do any of those complex things to end up living a simple life like he was. The wealthy man just stopped talking and realized what a foolish life he was leading, and remained silent for the rest of the trip. When he went home, he sold all of his things, bought a small house, and a small boat by the water and lived a long time as a simple, happy, and contented man.

SIMPLICITY PRACTICES

For you to begin to simplify your life, you need to start by envisioning and consciously connecting to a simpler, more natural aspect of life. You will be using the element of Earth for healing your challenges with complexity and material attachment, to reconnect to simplicity as a way of living. Take time every day to practice the art of simplicity. Find a special outdoor place to practice this.

Once there, take off your shoes and go barefoot if you can, socks at max. Sit on the ground for your 10-15 min sacred preparation exercise (on page 49) to release, ground and expand you.

Next open your eyes, stand up and begin to walk in your yard or around the park, the beach, or garden that you have found in your area.

Like a labyrinth walk continually in a pattern that you intuitively feel called to travel. Don't look up and around, only look down at your feet and look at everything there that is in front of you.

Listen deeply to the surrounding sounds of nature as it fills your listening space; savor the colors and shapes surrounding your visual experience.

Pick up things that you see, and look at them; feel the texture and contours of each piece that you engage with, but then put them down again. Do not take anything away with you.

Become very aware of the Earth beneath your feet and feel its vibration rising up through you. As you begin to resonate with its frequency your heart will cohere to the heartbeat of the Earth and you will relax, coming into a space of ease and well-being.

"Walk as if you are kissing the Earth with your feet."
-THICH NHAT HANH

When you walk in your bare feet, this becomes the practice of Earthing; connecting your life-force down into the core of the Earth, receiving Mother Earth's healing energy into your body, and then grounding yourself down into the Earth by returning the energy to her.

With this practice, you will begin to receive charged healing energy from Mother Earth everyday instead of man-made energy exchanges, material purchases, over-booked schedules, and doing to do. Savor the pure and powerful experience of the simple pleasures of Earth's energy. Begin to remember that you do not need "things," to feel ease and comfort, and say to yourself until you believe it, "I AM FREE when enjoying the simple things that the Earth naturally offers me." You now have a daily practice to pull yourself out of the complex rat race, recharge you with earth energy that will create a sense of simple balance and ease in your life. You begin to remember that sensory discovery experiences are what you are wanting, the feelings of this, not the things themselves. Your mind is satisfied and your life is simpler. Do not take anything home but memories!

You should do this every day for at least 20 minutes. If you can more than once a day. You can do it at home, on break at work, on your way home from work, or after dropping the kids off.

Find a place outside in each of the areas that you travel around to, so you can access one of the places on any given day.

By reminding your mind and body from a state of ease that life really is simple, you gain access to this unencumbered truth. Once you begin to put this knowing into your belief structure, replacing old beliefs that life is complex, you can have the health and harmony benefits of a lighter and simpler sacred life. At each session and throughout the day, repeat to yourself, "I AM free and at ease when life is simple," until you begin to feel it as truth inside of you!

JOURNEY #2
COMMENTS and CONCLUSIONS

After every session, as often as you can journal, record your experience; as a response, thought, feeling, problem, or achievement. Use words, pictures, note, or poetry to make your points, and look at them at least once a week. Journal about what your reflective-self has to say about the comments and as you go deeper and longer you will discover more and possibly excavate the root cause of your need for complexity in your life. This is a journey ultimately of self-discovery of your own process and perspectives on the path to sacred living, as well as developing your sacred-self.

Write on the following reflective questions:
DAY #1
1. Do I have beliefs that the world is complex and why?

2. Why and when do I chose complexity over simplicity?

3. What are new beliefs that I can live by that can foster simplicity in my life?

4. When I am earthing what value does it bring me? How does it make me feel? Does it help me to feel lighter?

5. How do I feel when I have a lighter schedule or no schedule at all?

DAY #2

1. Do I have beliefs that the world is complex and why?

2. Why and when do I chose complexity over simplicity?

3. What are new beliefs that I can live by that can foster simplicity in my life?

4. When I am earthing what value does it bring me? How does it make me feel? Does it help me to feel lighter?

5. How do I feel when I have a lighter schedule or no schedule at all?

DAY #3

1. Do I have beliefs that the world is complex and why?

2. Why and when do I chose complexity over simplicity?

3. What are new beliefs that I can live by that can foster simplicity in my life?

4. When I am earthing what value does it bring me? How does it make me feel? Does it help me to feel lighter?

5. How do I feel when I have a lighter schedule or no schedule at all?

DAY #4

1. Do I have beliefs that the world is complex and why?

2. Why and when do I chose complexity over simplicity?

3. What are new beliefs that I can live by that can foster simplicity in my life?

4. When I am earthing what value does it bring me? How does it make me feel? Does it help me to feel lighter?

5. How do I feel when I have a lighter schedule or no schedule at all?

DAY #5

1. Do I have beliefs that the world is complex and why?

2. Why and when do I chose complexity over simplicity?

3. What are new beliefs that I can live by that can foster simplicity in my life?

4. When I am earthing what value does it bring me? How does it make me feel? Does it help me to feel lighter?

5. How do I feel when I have a lighter schedule or no schedule at all?

DAY #6

1. Do I have beliefs that the world is complex and why?

2. Why and when do I chose complexity over simplicity?

3. What are new beliefs that I can live by that can foster simplicity in my life?

4. When I am earthing what value does it bring me? How does it make me feel? Does it help me to feel lighter?

5. How do I feel when I have a lighter schedule or no schedule at all?

DAY #7

1. Do I have beliefs that the world is complex and why?

2. Why and when do I chose complexity over simplicity?

3. What are new beliefs that I can live by that can foster simplicity in my life?

4. When I am earthing what value does it bring me? How does it make me feel? Does it help me to feel lighter?

5. How do I feel when I have a lighter schedule or no schedule at all?

CONCLUSIONS:

1. What am I taking off of my to-do list permanently?

2. What am I spending more time doing? Everyday? Every Week?

3. What are my new daily behavior patterns that are simpler and easier?

MY SIMPLICITY MANTRA

EARTH ENERGY CALMS ME AND BRINGS ME EASE

WHEN I DO ONE THING AT A TIME, ALL THINGS THAT ARE TRULY NECESSARY DO GET DONE

LIFE IS REALLY SIMPLE WHEN I SEE IT AS SUCH AND IT BRINGS ME LIGHTNESS OF BEING AND I FEEL FREE

Sink Into Surrender

SACRED HEALING JOURNEY #3
On the path from RESISTANCE ———→ FLOW "I AM LIGHT"

In modern society, *surrender* is seen as a position that is weak, defeated, copping out. Instead we use control behavior which is not seen as a sign of weakness. When under stress we use control to make ourselves feel comfortable. Unfortunately under stress the higher awareness part of ourselves literally shuts down so that our survival systems can activate fully and unimpeded…all energy, blood flow and thoughts are around how to resist or control our stressful situation by fighting or fleeing to survive. Because modern life is so constantly oriented around producing stress reactions, we feel like we have to rely on our survival instincts quite frequently, but we cannot from that survival place access unlimited Universal life force energy. As we continually control our outer circumstances as a means to obtain some comfort since we can't find and feel Universal life force FLOW we get even more stressed out.

We are in essence resisting the state of FLOW. Actually, when stressed, trusting in the Universe to provide and just letting go of control and going into the flow of Universal benevolence, gives us access to our higher mind so that we can heal our traumas and creatively live our lives easily, effortlessly, and stress free. Surrendering into life force FLOW, which is all around us, in us, and of us, brings us freedom to allow ourselves to review and release our emotional traumas and step into a lightness of being!

SURRENDER PRACTICES

To allow yourself to sink into surrender mode, you will first need to identify your control/resistance behavior patterns and find the flow/surrender energy equivalent. Using the element of inner fire, you will take the powerful energy of your personal will that fuels survival resistance/control behavior patterns, and you will replace it with the accompanying surrender/flow pattern.

The healing practice on this journey shows you how you can use fire energy from resistance/control patterns to springboard you into flow patterns that become light, fun, and free form; play, dance, song, laughter are all types of flow patterns. Identify one of the following resistance/control patterns active in your life, and choose to let it go and replace it with surrender flow behavior. Your beliefs will adjust too! We have the ability to change our beliefs and behaviors and rewire ourselves to enjoy the benefits of going with the Universal flow!

Control		Flow	
Resistance behaviors	Limiting Belief	Replacement Behaviors	Flow Belief
ANGER	I'm being controlled by another	LAUGHTER	When I surrender control, I FLOW
WORRY	I can't control my life	PLAY	When I surrender control, I FLOW
ANXIETY	I might be out of control	DEEP BREATHING	When I surrender control, I FLOW
TIGHTNESS	I am getting out of control	STRETCHING	When I release control, I FLOW
PUSHING	I need to be in control	LET GO	When I stop controlling, I FLOW
TELLING	I deserve to be in control	LISTEN	When I stop controlling others, I FLOW
RUNNING	I don't want to be controlled	STAY	When I surrender control, I FLOW
SHRINKING	I think that I can be controlled	OPEN	When I surrender control, I FLOW
PANIC	I am out of control	PRAY	When I surrender control, I FLOW
TURN OFF	I want to be in control	TUNE IN	When I surrender control, I FLOW

Take each opportunity to harness the powerful energy behind resistance/control patterns, and shift into surrender/FLOW behaviors as they arise throughout the day. Whenever your control pattern comes up, stop doing it and surrender into the Universal high vibrating energy that powers you with the power of the Universe through your Divine will. GO WITH THE FLOW.

Once you begin to release control you will be able to begin to look at your reasons for using control, the traumas that caused you to use control. Through conscious awareness of witnessing this without judgment you can begin to heal the old trauma, feeling happier and healthier. As you get further along on your healing journey let this be your playtime when you connect into it. Use the element of fire to ignite a more sacred version of our self. As you bring your Divine self into play and send it out into the world, say to yourself until you believe it, "I AM FREE" when I FLOW in the unlimited energies of The Universe!"

The surrender into FLOW process will also make it easier to be responsive versus reactive to any situation that triggers you going forward. Another very strong indicator that you are in surrender mode, is when you choose to pause and reflect instead of react to any challenging experience in front of you. The pause gives you the space to choose the higher pattern of FLOW/response instead of the limited pattern of control reaction. Surrender, pause, reflect, FLOW, and then respond more sacredly! Surrender, gifts you the space to do this.

JOURNEY #3
COMMENTS and CONCLUSIONS

After every session, as often as you can journal, record your experience; a response, thought, feeling, problem, achievement. Use words, pictures, note, or poetry to make your points and look at them at least once a week to see what your reflective self has to say about the comments. Journal again on these reflections. At the end of the month, review your weekly comments, and journal about them, going deeper into your understandings of self. As you engage longer with this process you will go deeper into the root cause of your trauma induced control pattern. This is a journey ultimately of self-discovery of your own process and perspectives on the path to sacred living as well as developing your sacred self.

PRACTICES OF REFLECTION ON THE JOURNEY TO SURRENDER

WEEK 1- What is the control/FLOW pattern you are observing?

As you observe your control pattern….

1. Ask yourself each time, why did I choose control in a given situation?

2. What is my belief about this situation?

3. How do I feel when I'm in control? not in control?

Practice the surrender response for that control behavior and observe yourself….

1. Ask yourself how it feels to be in FLOW vs control?

2. Was it hard to release control and why??

3. Do you prefer to be in control or FLOW?

4. Does it feel better, more relaxed, easier, healthier to use FLOW behavior then control?

WEEK 2- What is the control/FLOW pattern you are observing?

As you observe your control pattern....
1.Ask yourself each time, why did I choose control in a given situation?

2.What is my belief about this situation?

3.How do I feel when I'm in control? not in control?

Practice the surrender response for that control behavior and observe yourself....
1.Ask yourself how it feels to be in FLOW vs control?

2.Was it hard to release control and why??

3. Do you prefer to be in control or FLOW?

4.Does it feel better, more relaxed, easier, healthier to use FLOW behavior then control?

WEEK 3- What is the control/FLOW pattern you are observing?

As you observe your control pattern....
1.Ask yourself each time, why did I choose control in a given situation?

2.What is my belief about this situation?

3.How do I feel when I'm in control? not in control?

Practice the surrender response for that control behavior and observe yourself....
1.Ask yourself how it feels to be in FLOW vs control?

2.Was it hard to release control and why??

3. Do you prefer to be in control or FLOW?

4.Does it feel better, more relaxed, easier, healthier to use FLOW behavior then control?

WEEK 4- What is the control/FLOW pattern you are observing?

As you observe your control pattern....
1.Ask yourself each time, why did I choose control in a given situation?

2.What is my belief about this situation?

3.How do I feel when I'm in control? not in control?

Practice the surrender response for that control behavior and observe yourself....
1.Ask yourself how it feels to be in FLOW vs control?

2.Was it hard to release control and why??

3. Do you prefer to be in control or FLOW?

4.Does it feel better, more relaxed, easier, healthier to use FLOW behavior then control?

WEEK 5- What is the control/FLOW pattern you are observing?

As you observe your control pattern....
1.Ask yourself each time, why did I choose control in a given situation?

2.What is my belief about this situation?

3.How do I feel when I'm in control? not in control?

Practice the surrender response for that control behavior and observe yourself....
1.Ask yourself how it feels to be in FLOW vs control?

2.Was it hard to release control and why??

3. Do you prefer to be in control or FLOW?

4.Does it feel better, more relaxed, easier, healthier to use FLOW behavior then control?

WEEK 6- What is the control/FLOW pattern you are observing?

As you observe your control pattern....
1. Ask yourself each time, why did I choose control in a given situation?

2. What is my belief about this situation?

3. How do I feel when I'm in control? not in control?

Practice the surrender response for that control behavior and observe yourself....
1. Ask yourself how it feels to be in FLOW vs control?

2. Was it hard to release control and why??

3. Do you prefer to be in control or FLOW?

4. Does it feel better, more relaxed, easier, healthier to use FLOW behavior then control?

CONCLUSIONS:

I. Which control patterns did I give up and which FLOW patterns did I choose instead?

	GIVE UP	CHOOSE
1.		
2.		
3.		

II. Do a fire ceremony once you obtain total clarity on which control/resistance patterns you want to release and which surrender/FLOW patterns you want to adopt.

a. Make a small fire outside or light a candle inside

b. Place your control words on a small piece of paper and with sacred intent state that you are releasing this pattern from your life in gratitude

c. Place the slip of paper into the fire and as it burns acknowledge the flow pattern you have adopted to replace this control pattern and bring you into greater lightness of being

MY FLOW MANTRA:

RESISTANCE AND CONTROL OF A SITUATION BLOCKS AND CONSTRICTS MY ACCESS TO HEALING UNIVERSAL LIFE FORCE ENERGY, LIGHT AND LOVE

WHEN I RELEASE CONTROL AND LET GO INTO UNIVERSAL LIFE FORCE FLOW, I AM ABLE TO SEE WHAT IS LIMITING ME, HEAL AND CHOOSE A SACRED LIGHTER PATH, FREE FROM MY PAST TRAUMA THAT HAS BOUND ME!

BEGIN TO TRAVEL LIGHT!!

Stay Present

SACRED HEALING JOURNEY #4
On the path from WORRY ──────⟶ WONDER "I AM PEACEFUL"

Worry is such a strong but wasted energy and it can be harmful too. It is the intense focus on past discomfort, pain and problems, with a constant and simultaneous projecting of them possibly happening to you in your future. Social research has concluded that over 95% of what we worry about, NEVER comes true. We also know through the studies in quantum physics, what we focus on with our mind, give attention to with a strong similar frequency of feelings behind it, we create and make manifest. So, do we want to create all of the things we are worrying about? It is very important to remove worry from our behavior patterns! But how do we do that?

Worry comes from a lack of trust in the Universe. If we don't know that the Universe has been created so that our thoughts create our reality and that we are in control of our lives more then we realize, then we default to a blame cycle of outside forces. We see the world as hostile and unloving and believe that worry is caution and it will protect us from the outside marauders. Unfortunately, unless we are fully present in our moments, instead of in worry from fear that something might happen to us, we are unable to see and experience that the true nature and wonder of the Universe is designed to give us whatever we are wanting all of the time. In our worrying thoughts is also a lack of living in the present which is actually the way to having the peace that we are falsely seeking as relief through worry. Have faith and TRUST in the Universe to provide (by design) and when you practice using the tool of present moment awareness to release you from worry and fear you will find that the world is actually a wondrously, peaceful place.

"Don't worry about a thing... Cause every little thing gonna be alright."
- BOB MARLEY

Practices of meditation, prayer, drumming, dance, and chanting are scientifically proven to take you into present moment awareness and timelessness experiences, but there are also some sensory nature practices that are proven equally effective in releasing you from the past/future worry cycle and will connect you to your present peaceful moment... as Eckart Tolle would say, your NOW moment!

STAYING IN THE PRESENT PRACTICES

Using the element of air and the energy of the wind, explore sky gazing.

Go outside at least once a day and relax in a chair or lay down somewhere relaxing and look up at the sky where you have the sun, the clouds, the stars, the planets, and the moon. Anytime of the day or night, there is something stellar to gaze at.

Start out by doing your sacred preparation exercise (on page 49).

Next set your sites on the sky above you and don't take your eyes off the skies for at least 20 minutes in a session. Let your mind float away while you sit or lie down looking up at the clouds; be the observer fully, mindfully, and in pure presence.

Let your worries, thoughts and emotions, as they arise in your body and mind, just float right above you into the clouds, the stars, the moon, or the sun. Don't judge them or stay attached to them...let them GO!

Feel the air around you. Let the winds and breezes embrace you and surround you in comfort and protection. Stay mindful of the winds healing and comforting presence.

Connect to the wind energy and merge with it, and allow yourself to simply be an observer, completely immersed in each moment of experience and nothing else.

Stay with it until you feel a sense of wonder and awe seep into your being. At the end of the session, repeat many times to yourself until you believe it, "I AM PEACEFUL IN PURE PRESENCE."

What you will begin to observe after a session like this is that, if you remain open, as you re-enter the physical world fully, you will have a sense of deep peace and also access to your intuitive guidance system in a new way. You will be able to know where to go and what to do next, without giving thought to things. You will begin to look at all of life as wondrous and full of opportunity, all of the time. You will begin to see that your inner guidance system is far easier and superior to your mind in making decisions about daily life. The present mind and heart envisions creations in alignment with our higher-self.

The Universe always wants to send us our most benevolent outcome, but it's only by being fully present, that our most benevolent outcome can unfold for us. If we sit in a place of pure presence, we will take a wondrous journey to peace within.

JOURNEY #4
COMMENTS and CONCLUSIONS

After every session as often as you can journal, record your experience; a response, thought, feeling, problem, or achievement. Use words, pictures, note, or poetry to make your points, and look at them at least once a week to see what your reflective-self has to say about these comments. As you practice staying present longer you will go deeper into your inner truths and be able to see root causes of traumas and joys more readily. This is a journey ultimately of self-discovery of your own process and perspectives on the path to sacred living as well as developing your sacred-self.

Sky Gazing daily reflective journaling:

Date:

Which Sky Gazing Activity did I choose?

1.What was the effect of sky gazing on me?

2. How long did it take me to get into pure presence and leave past and future behind?

3. Did I use sky gazing at any other points throughout the day to reset myself into the present moment?

4. Did I feel more peaceful in pure presence and how long was I able to stay there in that state of present moment?

5. Am I connecting to my intuition when I'm in pure presence?

6. What is my intuition telling me to do differently in my day to day life?

Date:
Which Sky Gazing Activity did I choose?

1. What was the effect of sky gazing on me?

2. How long did it take me to get into pure presence and leave past and future behind?

3. Did I use sky gazing at any other points throughout the day to reset myself into the present moment?

4. Did I feel more peaceful in pure presence and how long was I able to stay there in that state of present moment?

5. Am I connecting to my intuition when I'm in pure presence?

6. What is my intuition telling me to do differently in my day to day life?

Date:
Which Sky Gazing Activity did I choose?

1.What was the effect of sky gazing on me?

2. How long did it take me to get into pure presence and leave past and future behind?

3. Did I use sky gazing at any other points throughout the day to reset myself into the present moment?

4. Did I feel more peaceful in pure presence and how long was I able to stay there in that state of present moment?

5. Am I connecting to my intuition when I'm in pure presence?

6. What is my intuition telling me to do differently in my day to day life?

Date:
Which Sky Gazing Activity did I choose?

1.What was the effect of sky gazing on me?

2. How long did it take me to get into pure presence and leave past and future behind?

3. Did I use sky gazing at any other points throughout the day to reset myself into the present moment?

4. Did I feel more peaceful in pure presence and how long was I able to stay there in that state of present moment?

5. Am I connecting to my intuition when I'm in pure presence?

6. What is my intuition telling me to do differently in my day to day life?

Date:
Which Sky Gazing Activity did I choose?

1.What was the effect of sky gazing on me?

2. How long did it take me to get into pure presence and leave past and future behind?

3. Did I use sky gazing at any other points throughout the day to reset myself into the present moment?

4. Did I feel more peaceful in pure presence and how long was I able to stay there in that state of present moment?

5. Am I connecting to my intuition when I'm in pure presence?

6. What is my intuition telling me to do differently in my day to day life?

Date:
Which Sky Gazing Activity did I choose?

1.What was the effect of sky gazing on me?

2. How long did it take me to get into pure presence and leave past and future behind?

3. Did I use sky gazing at any other points throughout the day to reset myself into the present moment?

4. Did I feel more peaceful in pure presence and how long was I able to stay there in that state of present moment?

5. Am I connecting to my intuition when I'm in pure presence?

6. What is my intuition telling me to do differently in my day to day life?

CONCLUSIONS:

1.Is sky gazing a good practice for me or did I find another practice along the way to help me release worrying thoughts and to get into and stay in pure presence?

2. Why is pure presence and staying/ living in the present moment good for my health and for others around me?

MY PEACE MANTRA

I AM COMMITTED TO STAYING PRESENT WHEN DOING TASKS, LISTENING TO OTHERS, PLAYING, EATING, AND WORKING.

IF I AM WORRYING, OVER THINKING OR HANGING ON TO EMOTING, I RECOGNIZE THAT I AM IN THE PAST OR THE FUTURE... LIVING IN STRESS, LIMITATION, FEAR OR ANGUISH. I CHOOSE INSTEAD TO OBSERVE MY WORRYING EMOTIONS OBJECTIVELY AND I CHOOSE TO RELEASE THESE EMOTIONS THAT NO LONGER SERVE ME.

IF I CAN'T RELEASE FROM MY NEGATIVE, WORRYING MIND OR EMOTIONS, I WILL STOP AND GAZE AT THE MAJESTIC SKY IN WONDER TO RESET MYSELF TO THE PRESENT NOW MOMENT IN FRONT OF ME.

IN THE PRESENT MOMENT, TIME DOES NOT EXIST, LIFE FORCE IS FULLY AVAILABLE TO ME, I EXPERIENCE THE WONDERS OF THE UNIVERSE ALWAYS RIGHT IN FRONT OF ME, IF I AM JUST PRESENT ENOUGH TO SEE IT, AND MY HEART WILL LEAD THE WAY.

Share Your Gifts
SACRED HEALING JOURNEY #5

On the path from CONTRIVED ⟶ ALIVE "I AM EMPOWERED"

We begin our life journey as children, greatly influenced by those around us, and the culture that we grow up in. We like to please, because it brings us less discomfort and occasionally praise, so we begin early on to conform to other standards of what they think we should do, what they think is right and wrong, and who we are. We most often follow others ideas on our path to our jobs and their life choices for us, sometimes until we die. Most people on this planet are not living the life of their authentic self; their life is a contrived lie.

If we were all meant to be the same, we would have been created the same, but that is not the reality. We are as individually unique as snowflakes. We each have a unique set of energetic imprints, with a path to follow and a purpose to sow here on earth. The first task is remembering this truth, that we are individual God/Source created uniqueness. The second task, is the personal awakening to the truth of who WE are. As children, we come in with this knowing until adults overlay their perspectives, so we need to get very childlike in exploring the reawakening of our unique-self.

The discovery of the unique authentic-self, creates a sense of excitement in our being. When we feel the truth of who we are and we put it out there in the world, the feelings of "aliveness" become our cue to remind us, that we are on the path of the authentic-self, and it is our guidepost for staying on this path. When we are "alive" we are aligned, energized and empowered to do most anything we need or want to do!

PRACTICES FOR DISCOVERING AND SHARING OUR GIFTS

Take a retreat day, or ideally a weekend and go off on your own into a nature setting to relax, simplify, surrender your material responsibilities, and get into pure presence. If you can, go to a retreat center or to a cabin in the woods, a cottage in the country, or to a beach get away. Bring this notebook and old photo albums for lots of writing and journaling at your retreat space.

Once you are settled in, take an hour to engage in sacred practices #1-4. Ground yourself in solitude, get into the serenity of simplicity, surrender your will and agendas for outcomes of anything specific and come fully into the present moment. Use the sacred preparation exercise (on page 49) to start to help you anchor in these 4 sacred practices: the ocean meditation, earthing and sky gazing exercises plus activating your FLOW activity.

After the first hour of sacred preparation activities you should feel relaxed, present and self-aware of your access to being in the FLOW of life force energy. You and the Universe will co-create this next process together!

The discovery process of the "authentic self" is similar to a Japanese process used to determine, "your reason for being" ...Ikigai...." a reason to get up in joy every morning," a path to feeling alive. Through deep inner research, you can uncover a life path that features your uniquely combined gifts, passions, and purpose into a new job, hobby, service offering, play project, or creative endeavor.

JOURNEY # 5

At each journal session use words, pictures, note, or poetry to make your points and look at them at least once a week to see what your reflective self has to say about the comments. This is a journey ultimately of self-discovery of your own process and perspectives on the path to sacred living as well as developing your sacred- self.

Discovering your Unique Purpose and Self

The discovery phase- Start out by making a list of all the things you have accomplished in your life to date in every aspect of your life (go through those old photo albums first for reminders).

Step 1: Decade LIFE REVIEW - List 10 accomplishments in each decade of your life that reflected your gifts, skills, talents, abilities, things that you did that motivated, inspired, or excited others while you were happy or having fun while doing it.

0-10 YEARS
1.
2.
3.
4.
5.
6.
7.
8.
9.
10.

11-20 YEARS
1.
2.
3.
4.
5.
6.
7.
8.
9.
10.

21-30 YRS
1.
2.
3.
4.

5.

6.

7.

8.

9.

10.

31-40 YEARS

1.

2.

3.

4.

5.

6.

7.

8.

9.

10.

41-50 YEARS

1.

2.

3.

4.

5.

6.

7.

8.

9.

10.

51-60 YEARS

1.

2.

3.

4.

5.

6.

7.

8.

9.

10.

61-70 YEARS

1.

2.

3.

4.

5.

6.

7.

8.

9.

10.

70-80 YEARS AND BEYOND

1.

2.

3.

4.

5.

6.

7.

8.

9.

10.

Step 2: ALIVE List - Choose 10 things off of the lists above that still make you feel alive while thinking about or envisioning them.

1.
2.
3.
4.
5.
6.
7.
8.
9.
10.

NOTES :

Step 3: IN SERVICE to others List—Choose 5 things from the list above that you do well and that make you feel alive that are in service to others.

1.
2.
3.
4.
5.

NOTES:

Step 4: EXCITEMENT List- Choose 3 things off the previous list that make you feel excited when you envision them happening in your life.

1.

2.

3.

NOTES:

Step 5: YOUR REASON FOR BEING or AUTHENTIC PURPOSE- Choose one thing from above that brings you great joy and gives you a reason to get up every morning feeling ALIVE!!!

1.

General NOTES:

Step 6: Make a PLAN to get your authentic self and purpose out there ASAP... begin the process this week!!!

A PLAN for putting your Unique Purpose and Authentic Self out in the world

GOALS	STRATEGIES	SUPPORT TEAM
(what to do)	(when, where and how to do it)	(who to help and support you with it)
I.		
II.		
III.		

There can be several challenges when you re-identify and engage your authentic self with others; some will not like the changes, and you will have to develop courage and strength to stand your ground and let others possibly slip away from your life. When you are authentically expressing yourself, some people may try to put you down and deter you from changing. You need to surround yourself with those people that support your new journey. When you are faced with a choice to engage in your authentic path and other's paths that intersect yours prove in conflict, do not defer to them, instead claim your path, purpose, and dialogue about finding a way to express yourself with the others simultaneously.

PROBLEMS TO WATCH OUT FOR....

What if there are problems along the way to expressing your authentic self out in the world????....

What happens when others don't support you as your authentic self?

What happens when others try to block you from sharing your authentic self, yourself included?

What do you do when others expect you to sacrifice yourself for them? Do you stand your authentic ground, assuring that your needs are met alongside of others?!

Be the one to stand up for yourself and teach others to do the same by example. When all human beings are shining their light, while in service to each other, then the world shines brighter for all! When you are aligned as your authentic-self in body, mind, heart, and spirit, you will feel alive! Sing your song loudly, as the world needs each tune to create the planetary symphony!!

WRITING YOUR SOUL SONG

Once you remember what makes you feel alive and start living it, turn your reason for being into a personal mantra, turn it into your soul song; your own song that speaks of your unique wisdom, talents and beauty. Begin to see yourself as a vibration, a frequency, a sound.

A. What kind of music do you sound like when you feel alive with the vibe of YOU?

B. What is the name of your soul song? Song title?

C. Give it a melody line or use and familiar one and sing it to yourself throughout the day suggesting to yourself that your gifts are your power and are important to share.

D. Write a series of lyrics to your soul song.

E. Immerse yourself in your soul song for 30 minutes every day until, you have manifested and stepped into your authentic, powerful you. Say to yourself, "I AM POWERFUL, and I have important work to do out in the world," until you believe it!!

CONCLUSIONS:

1. My reason for being is...

2. My soul song title is...

MY AUTHENTIC SELF MANTRA

I AM AWARE THAT IF I AM NOT LIVING AS MY AUTHENTIC SELF, THAT I AM DENYING MYSELF AND MY PLANETARY FAMILY OF MY FULL LIGHT AND GIFTS EXPRESSED IN THE WORLD AS ME...."TO THINE OWN SELF BE TRUE"

AS I CHOOSE TO LIVE AS MY AUTHENTIC SELF, I AM EMPOWERED TO LIVE MY FULLEST LIFE, ALIVE IN EVERY WAY, EVERY DAY

THE EXPRESSION OF MY AUTHENTIC SELF IS MY SERVICE TO OTHERS AND IS MY WAY TO FULFILL MY PURPOSE ON THE PLANET TO MAKE THE WORLD A BETTER PLACE FOR MYSELF AND EVERYONE ON IT.

Sit In Joy

SACRED HEALING JOURNEY #6
On the path from MUNDANE ⟶ MAGICAL "I AM GRATEFUL

How do you find joy and sustain it in a modern world where suffering, sadness and stress are so prevalent every day? Oddly enough, you have to first release the mind from its mundane, negative thoughts that are filled with what is wrong, not working, is upsetting, listing all the things that you don't have or that aren't "right". Full of judgment, blame, regret and remorse, our minds co create and reinforce this worldview and we begin to see this version of the world as the way that life is...and so that is what you experience...a suffering life.

To start to move into the joy realms you have to let that all go, all that negative mundane chatter, and replace it with magical, positive, joy filled thoughts, feelings, words, and images. The first journey to joy is an inner one. Learn to think, feel, vision and speak of what you love, you have, what is working, what is beautiful, what you are grateful for. Don't think about the painful thoughts, feelings, and circumstances that are upsetting you. Why would you want to create more of these experiences in your life?! Create your life experiences through your appreciative thoughts and emotions and enjoy the joy energy you feel in your body in return. What we give sustained focus on with desire, we manifest. It works like magic every time! This is the Universal design.

We sadly do not allow ourselves to spend time in our joyous thoughts and choices as we should. We are trained to work as hard as we can in the modern world, doing whatever it takes to get to our material goals. We define joy often as the acquisition of material things or an extracurricular activity which sometimes gets airtime. We go from a fleeting joyful experience back to mundane thoughts and experiences and then feeling empty or bored, we refocus on joy to make us feel better. But because it is not a core value of humans in modern society, we keep forgetting its importance, do not stay focused on joy and we let it go. Our lives therefore remain greatly lacking in joy...unless we choose to stay there!!!

We have ways to generate and create more joy in our life; with our outer world choices, such as who, what, when, and where we want to spend our time.

Most people die without even making their bucket list, let alone living it. With all the hours of all the days we have here in a lifetime, if you knew that you were going to die tomorrow and had the choice, would you spend so much of it in joyless thoughts and pursuits? Do we ever really know how much time is ours to enjoy on this beautiful planet of ours? And if or when we actually get to that joy filled state of being, do we sit in that joy, or do we move right through it and refocus on our problems, pain, and discomforts?

We need to make joy a priority in our lives and quest to explore and discover this part of ourselves and bring it to life in our lives so that we live fully and magically every day. A good place to start this journey is to search for and recognize the joy already within and around us and then to commit to sitting in it more and more often every day of our life.

PRACTICES IN SEARCH OF OUR JOY

If you can, get away and craft an afternoon or day for yourself to indulge in the discovery of the things, thoughts, experiences, and attitudes that bring you joy. At the very least, try to be in a quiet alone space for several hours, start there. Then get out old photo albums, favorite magazines, scissors, and glue sticks and begin by looking through these resources at all of your favorite things and cut them out. You are going to make a collage/storyboard/ vision JOY board to put up in your home.

Start out by sitting or lying on a comfortable chair outdoors for your first hour of this activity. Use the sacred preparation exercise (on page 49) to start to get you relaxed. When you begin to fall into that, "napping state" and get to feeling "dreamy" allow yourself to begin to open up to your imagination with the intention of only wanting to feel joy. Plan to hang out in this dream state for an hour or so.

Have this journal by your side and jot down whatever starts to come up to your conscious mind. When you start to envision things that make you feel joyful, expand, on the experience. Play around with it in your mind until you create a scene of experiences that feel joyful. Write them all down.

Next get up and go to a table and leaf through a series of magazines and start to cut out all of the things that make you feel joyful, excited, alive, happy, blissful. This can be people, places, things, songs, colors, words. How do these things taste to you, smell, feel to the touch? Put those words on top of some blank pages in your sacred journal, and then cut out the words or write them on your collage over top of your pictures of joy. If you can find pictures or words or images that capture your daydreams, cut those out as well.

Then take the completed collage that you put on an 8x10 piece of cardboard, frame it and place it by your bed, on a wall that you look at in bed, or on a stand on your night table. Contemplate on it when you awaken, and at night before you go to sleep. Look at it and feel the joy of experience from each picture and word and sit in the feelings that are elicited for at least ten minutes at night and each morning. As you feel the joy, name it and claim the feelings for it is not what we are wanting to do often that brings us joy, but it is what we feel from an experience of joy.

We, therefore, need to see the feeling separate from the event. We want to hold the feeling that we are wanting from the past joyful memory, and let it be the magnetic frequency of attraction for our next manifestation, thus maintaining that joy feeling as our continued experiences. As Esther Hicks often says, "manifest what you are wanting to feel, that is really what you are wanting."

Next, whenever any joyful feeling appears in response to your interactions with people, places, feelings, events in your life or in real time, sit in the experience of that reality for at least 30 minutes. Do not leave, do not think, do not talk; just sit and experience the magical feeling of those joyful moments!

JOURNEY #6

While journaling, use words, pictures, note, or poetry to make your points, and look at them at least once a week to see what your reflective-self has to say about these comments. This is a journey ultimately of self-discovery of your own process and perspectives on the path to sacred living as well as developing your sacred-self.

Project #1
Daydream Journaling

Make notes from your daydream session today. You can keep doing daydreaming sessions and allow those experience to continue to inform you and connect you to the joy that you wish to feel in your life. Record how these experiences look, taste to you, smell, feel to the touch as reflections and images of inner and outer joyfulness

Day Dream Notes on JOY
Session #1

Session #2

Session #3

Project #2
Making the JOY Collage

1. At a table, leaf through a series of magazines and start to cut out all of the things that make you feel joyful, excited, alive, happy, blissful.... This can be people, places, things, songs, colors, words.

2. Use your 8x10 cardboard piece as a canvas to paste your images and create your written exposé overlay. Fill it with your joy images once you locate them, Paste and draw them over a full page that you will later frame.

3. Put words that describe your joy FEELINGS on your collage over top of your pictures of joy. Put notes from your daydream reflections around and on the collage as well:

Project #3
Joy Journaling when sitting in front of your JOY collage or in real life Joyful experiences

Increase the time you spend in joyful thoughts, feelings and experiences each day. Be mindful of your joy moments throughout the day and keep a journal on the content and amount of time you spend in each experience. Make a commitment to increase your time spent by 5 minutes every time you are in the next joy filled experience over the next 1-2 months.

As an Example:

Walking in the state park after work feeling relaxed	10 minutes
Walking in the county park with dogs enjoying flowers	25 minutes

List Joy Experience   Time Spent

List Joy Experience   Time Spent

List Joy Experience   Time Spent

List Joy Experience   Time Spent

List Joy Experience   Time Spent

List Joy Experience   Time Spent

List Joy Experience   Time Spent

Project#4
Gratitude Journaling

Increase an Attitude of Gratitude... Everyday record or say to yourself thank you Creator for the experiences of joy in life and then note your appreciation on that which you are engaging with (people, pets, property, plants, the planet). Use the gratitude journal below just for this purpose, to help you focus and build your sense of joy and ability to live a magical life by choosing appreciation feelings and gratitude expressions and sitting in them every day.

Gratitude Entry- Write down what am I grateful for and then state my appreciation by telling someone about it

#1

#2

#3

#4

#5

#6

#7

#8

#9

#10

#11

#12

Project #5
Share your joy with others

Share your joy with others by expressing and sharing your joyful feelings when around and with others. This most often raises others up, but it can occasionally upset people who are anchored in suffering....but just keep on, keeping on. We each are only responsible for our own healing and expressions. Love everyone on their path to greater self-awareness, but don't let others knock you off of yours.

Day 1
Record below how it felt to share your appreciation and joy with others?

How did others respond to you?

Did it change how you joyfully expressed yourself?

Day 2
Record below how it felt to share your appreciation and joy with others?

How did others respond to you?

Did it change how you joyfully expressed yourself?

Day 3
Record below how it felt to share your appreciation and joy with others?

How did others respond to you?

Did it change how you joyfully expressed yourself?

Day 4
Record below how it felt to share your appreciation and joy with others?

How did others respond to you?

Did it change how you joyfully expressed yourself?

CONCLUSIONS:

Buy and keep a gratitude journal to record receiving wonderful experiences, opportunities, synchronicities, lessons and teachings in your life whenever and however they occur ongoing. You can be thankful for all that IS working in your life, the people that support you, the things that you do have, for food, water, breathe and life itself; for is that not something to be grateful for.

When we send that gratitude and joy energy out into the world by putting into the written as well as the spoken word, as the frequency of joy, we vibrate at some of the highest Divine energy on the planet. By emanating it out into the Universal field of consciousness, we raise our frequency, our friends, families, communities and the planetary frequency as well.

MY JOY MANTRA

I FULLY BECOME THE JOY THAT I AM WANTING TO EXPERIENCE AS I DO A DEEP DIVE DAILY INTO MY JOY MOMENTS.

WHEN I FEEL JOY FULLY INSIDE MYSELF, I CHOOSE TO STAY IN IT, ENJOYING IT AND APPRECIATING THE EXPERIENCE,

I SAY EACH TIME I EXPERIENCE JOY, "I AM GRATEFUL FOR THESE JOY FILLED MOMENTS IN MY LIFE," I SAY THIS REPEATEDLY TO MYSELF AND TO OTHERS WHO ARE WITH ME, KNOWING THAT IT IS ALREADY SO.

IN JOY, MY LIFE NOW LOOKS MORE LIKE A MAGICAL REALM THEN A MUNDANE ONE.

Source Love From The Source

SACRED HEALING JOURNEY #7
On the path from LIMITED ⟶ INFINITE - "I AM UNLIMITED LOVE"

Feel the LOVE of Infinite Source Energy in Nature…. The Source is Living Energy comprised of Conscious Intelligent Awareness, Unconditional LOVE in a field of Unlimited Creative Potential. Everything on Earth is living energy made up of these same properties and that includes us and Nature. We just need to believe that and align within our body, mind and heart to resonate as the frequency of that Source Energy. We do this most effectively when we are living as our sacred self. One way to move into our sacred nature, is by being in Nature more often. In Nature we feel, remember and connect to our own spiritually infinite Divineness. We experience the Source that created us and the consciousness of Mother Earth and all of the sentient beings upon her. Source Energy emanates through us immediately when we immerse ourselves in natures' wisdom, beauty and love.

In modern times, as we've become over focused and entrenched in the material world, we've became disconnected from our Source awareness. We've also lost our connection to Mother Earth and all the Nature beings, our closest and deepest allies in this journey that we call life on Earth.

To get reconnected and receive daily insight, healing, love and wisdom from Source through Nature we must engage again, fully present and aware, in direct experiences every day. At least once a day, go into your yard, the woods, a park and find a tree and sit under it, like the Buddha under the bodhi tree or as Jesus did in the Garden of a Gethsemane …they meditated, connected to Source Creator in nature and received wisdom, healing and personal power.

Take a forest bath daily and raise your energy vibration so that you can connect to the Infinite sacred nature within you and to the Cosmic Creator It's known as shinrin-yoku, or "forest bathing" in Japan. It's the practice of spending prolonged periods of time with trees in order to gain from their many health benefits.

"When you walk into a forest, science has now explained a part of that sacred experience. We now know that the aerosols produced by the forest actually do uplift your mood and affect your brain through your immune system"
-SCIENCE NEWS

Although there are many scientific articles which speak to the many health benefits of 'forest bathing' - one only has to reflect on one's own experience. Who hasn't felt an inner sense of well-being when stepping into a forest, or just into a small grove of trees in the country or a park? It is like pushing a life reset button, reestablishing a connection with our deepest most infinite self. It's hard not to feel something viscerally meaningful as we surround ourselves by trees, away from the artificial sounds and smells of indoor modern life.

Go into the forest and allow yourself to bathe in its healing powers consciously, intentionally...merging and allowing the creative Source of all creation to move through you and in you, as you. As you sit in the fullness of Mother Natures' forest or glen, in a wooded area or under a tree in your yard or park, stay there for as long as it takes... bring yourself into resonance with Source energy and connect to your divine higher infinite self through tree energy and consciousness.

As you sit with the trees, the mighty keepers of time and ancient knowledge, tap into their strength and wisdom. Go up to a tree thank it, and yes hug it, and then lay with your back against it and let it speak to you energetically as a conduit of The Unlimited Source of LOVE and WISDOM. With conscious awareness and intention, as you sit in communion with the forest kingdom you deeply connect into nature and come out healed and more spiritually imbued and possibly feeling and knowing that you are unconditionally loved as well!

"With their roots in the earth and their crowns in the heavens, trees connect these two planes of existence, integrating what is above with what is below. On an energetic level, trees perform the spiritual purpose of assisting all beings to evolve to a higher state of consciousness. Trees and forests are a prerequisite for life on our planet, they are the lungs of the earth. They functionally provide us with food, shelter, medicine and shade for water sustenance".
-PLATBOS MUSINGS

What could be more important or more in need of protecting than our forests. Plant some trees in your yard or community whenever you can and enjoy their spiritual, healing, health and life sustaining benefits every day!

FOREST BATHING DAILY PRACTICE

After you find your place under or next to a tree or trees, sit or lay down and begin by closing your eyes and relaxing using the sacred preparation exercise (on page 49). Next intentionally open yourself to receiving the forest energies letting them naturally surround you and wash over you for several minutes, clearing your energy field so that you can connect to infinite Source Creation. Open your eyes and observe each tree, each blade of grass, each flower, each bird that sings, each animal that passes you. Listen to and speak to the nature spirit in all things. Truly begin a dialogue of asking, in thought or word, and receive answers and information contained in the Source wisdom sent back to you that is within every element and being within nature, the GOD in all things.

Whenever you engage in forest bathing, breathe the energies of the forest in and out saying to yourself until you believe it "I AM INFINITE AND UNCONDITIONALLY LOVED by the Source of All Creation".

End your session using the sacred love path practice before departing:

The SACRED LOVE Path Practice

L. Look through the eyes of your heart and see everything and everyone though your soul ...see the divine in everything as you rest your gaze on each piece of nature surrounding you.

O. Open your mind and expand it as far as you can see ...take off the lid of thinking and go beyond to access universal mind and wisdom and the consciousness of the Creator, letting your intuition flow through you and guide you. Ask questions and listen for answers.

V. Value everything you see for in everything there is something for you...a teaching, an opportunity, a lesson, a roadmap, a new possibility ....every person ... every experience...every being is made up of the energy of the Universe ...the energy of LOVE.

E. Embrace each moment in presence and experience yourself in the flow of the universe and all of its divineness and don't forget to enjoy it!

Love is the substance of all life... This is the energy of creation... It is infinite... It is benevolent... It is joyful!

LOVE is the way, the truth, and the light...in that word contains all of the wisdom of the universe, all of the solutions to our problems, all of the paths to peace, all of the ways to health.... it is the most important piece of the sacred path. Our goal as sacred travelers is remembering, accessing and eventually vibrating as divine infinite love!! Feel the LOVE, become the LOVE, BE LOVE, I AM LOVE!

JOURNEY #7
NATURE JOURNALING

At each session use words, pictures, notes or poetry to make your points and look at them at least once a week to see what your reflective self has to say about the comments. This is a journey ultimately of self- discovery of your own process and perspectives on the path to sacred living as well as developing your sacred self.

After emptying and then expanding your mind, connect with Nature and Source energy by doing your Sacred Love Path practice. Engage consciously and sensorily until you feel a sense of merging with nature and Source. Record your experience each day. Increase your time until you get to a state of Oneness with All. The hope would be that you eventually will have a visceral experience of your infinite nature in Mother Natures' forests which is the final Cosmic journey...that of blissful Wonder!

Using this Nature Journal, record at the end of your experience each time about your thoughts, emotions, body sensations and note if you feel more connected to the trees, Mother Earth and/or Source Creation by answering the 3 questions after each session. Also record any visions, insights or information that are revealed to you.

FOREST BATHING JOURNAL
SESSION 1: Journal on...what did I feel? what did I think? what did I learn? from my nature experience today while I went forest bathing. Did I feel more loved and connected to the trees, Mother Earth /or Source Creation?

SESSION 2: Journal on…what did I feel? what did I think? what did I learn? from my nature experience today while I went forest bathing Did, I feel more loved and connected to the trees, Mother Earth /or Source Creation?

SESSION 3: Journal on…what did I feel? what did I think? what did I learn? from my nature experience today while I went forest bathing Did, I feel more loved and connected to the trees, Mother Earth /or Source Creation?

SESSION 4: Journal on…what did I feel? what did I think? what did I learn? from my nature experience today while I went forest bathing Did, I feel more loved and connected to the trees, Mother Earth /or Source Creation?

SESSION 5: Journal on...what did I feel? what did I think? what did I learn? from my nature experience today while I went forest bathing Did, I feel more loved and connected to the trees, Mother Earth /or Source Creation?

SESSION 6: Journal on...what did I feel? what did I think? what did I learn? from my nature experience today while I went forest bathing Did, I feel more loved and connected to the trees, Mother Earth /or Source Creation?

SESSION 7: Journal on...what did I feel?, what did I think?, what did I learn? from my nature experience today while I went forest bathing Did I feel more loved and connected to the trees, Mother Earth /or Source Creation?

CONCLUSIONS:

Did I reach a sense of oneness with everything around me?

Did I feel feelings of wonder, aliveness, relaxation or delight while in the forest?

Did I get connected to a Source of creation, myself or the force of Mother Nature?

MY LOVE MANTRA

I AM UNCONDITIONALLY LOVED ALL OF THE TIME AS I AM SURROUNDED BY NATURE AND CAN EXPERIENCE THIS TRUTH WHENEVER I SIMPLY, IN PURE PRESENCE, RESIDE THERE CONNECTED TO SOURCE AND EVERYONE AND EVERYTHING

WHEN I CONNECT WITH SOURCE, I BECOME MORE RELAXED AND PRESENT AND JOYFUL WHILE THERE. I AM ABLE TO LOVE EVERYONE, FORGIVE EVERYONE AND RECOGNIZE EVERYONE AS ME, AS I MERGE WITH THE COSMOS AND EVERYTHING IN IT, FOR WE ARE ALL ONE!

I AM WITNESSED, NURTURED, LOVED AND TRANSMUTED BY SOURCE WHILE SPENDING TIME IN NATURE AND COMMIT IN GRATITUDE TO THIS SACRED EXPERIENCE EVERY DAY.
I AM DIVINE, LOVE, LIGHT, PEACE, HARMONY

FINAL SHARINGS

1.Seek Solitude... If you are in fear then there is no trust in the Universe to provide... fear not... know that you are the creator of your own reality, and a master manifestor and trust that the Universe is designed to always provide you with everything you ask for and focus on...Spend enough time in solitude to allow this truth reveal itself to you grounding your thoughts, beliefs and body in Universal Laws and Truths. This is a sacred path.

2. Savor Simplicity... If you are overwhelmed it is because you believe that more material things are the solution to your life's problems...that it will bring you happiness. This struggle is a part of human life but discomfort is truly just information...it can wake you up and help you grow and see where your material world is really not serving you. Then you can just let it go a bit and lighten up your load by simplifying your life and stepping out of the material world as the only reality and step back into the spiritual one. This is a sacred path.

3. Sink into Surrender....If you are in anger or resistance, there is no flow, no peace operating within you... because you are in separation, not believing in the connectivity of everything to everyone else so you try to control everything and everyone ....and the truth is we are all from the same Source ....take care of your neighbor for he is you. Don't let your emotions control you and in return look to control others...You are more than this, you are a creator being, not a victim. NEUTRALIZE EMOTIONS and take the higher ground. Release resistance patterns and the need to control and move into a lighter place of being. Sink into surrender feeling free.... ACCEPTING and ALLOWING yourself to be in the easy and effortless FLOW of the Universe as a sacred path.

4. Stay Present... If you are upset, overwhelmed or unclear it is because you are not present. When you are present and living only in the moment of each moment, living in the NOW, divine wisdom comes through you immediately, it animates and informs you and allows you to move intuitively through your world with total clarity and direction for your highest and most benevolent outcome and for those around you as well. EXPAND beyond space and time and live in the world of unlimited potential, peacefully present as a sacred path.

5. Share your Gifts... If you are in judgment then you are not accepting that all beings are a unique spark of God and all have their own path and part to play just as you do... until you walk in another's moccasins you will never truly know or understand their journey...Don't waste your precious time and energy looking out at another and judging another.... use your life experiences to guide you and inform you about your authentic nature and higher self and the truth of what you're here to do. ALLOWING others their walk, while you walk yours fully is a sacred path.

6. Sit in Joy...If you are in pain or depression you are attached to suffering. Suffering is a choice, joy is a choice. Our attitudes and perspectives as a free will human are our choice ...do not forget this and live with the joy of this knowing and all will be well. "We are powerful beyond measure". Detach from the pain of the victim and refocus on becoming empowered by joy. Choose joy over pain and linger in those places of joy until you are filled with the light of bliss on this sacred path.

7. Source LOVE from the Source... If are sad because others are unkind or hurtful, know that you are loved by the Source/Great Spirit/Creator/God always...that YOU too are love ..... that love is all there is ...love is all there is .... love is all there is....love is all there is....... true LOVE from the Source, it has no beginning it has no end, it is unconditional, it is everlasting, it is everywhere. You simply need to open to it and allow it into your life.....Walk the path of sacred LOVE!!

By following these seven sacred paths: seeking solitude, simplicity and surrender, staying present, sharing self, sitting in joy and sourcing love from the Source, you will be SACREDLY LIVING every day!!! A'ho and so it is!

SACRED LIFESTYLE ROUTINES

The many ways to break in your day Sacredly .... a sample of my personal daily sacred lifestyle routines and rituals.

THE MORNING ROUTINE

Set up the first part of your day sacredly by clearing, nourishing, balancing and energizing your body mind and heart. Start your day with 6/15 minute sacred times during your standard morning routine. If you are mindfully in solitude, doing these practices will help you to raise your vibrational frequency to a level of well-being for yourself and to the benefit of everyone around you for the rest of the day!

1.When you open your eyes and your mind starts to turn around on the days' events, take advantage of that thought awareness and switch it to a few moments of gratitude. Think of five things that are working in your life, you are grateful for, you give thanks for. You can think on it as an intention, an affirmation, as a thought. What's important is to acknowledge the gifts, feel the appreciation and speak from a place of gratitude in your mind or verbally. This begins to reset your mental energetic body into sacred vibrations. I also speak my affirmation mantra and daily visionary oneness and other prayers at this time.

2. Next take a few moments while you're still lying in bed and reset some of your physical body by stretching the body and spine out so that toxins release out of your body that have been laying there not circulated at night and your muscles get stimulated with oxygen so that you can move more nimbly and aligned once you get out of bed. If you do yoga, go for it, even a simple 15 minute routine version!

3.As you put your feet on the ground, thank the element of earth. Breathe in from the Source and send Source energy down through your body and ground that energy into the Earth further preparing yourself to move centered through the day in continual higher vibrations. Stop for a few minutes and look at your JOY collage and begin to feel the emotional JOY that you are and will be creating today. Sit in it for a few...

4. Once you get into the bathroom for your morning routine, go in with intention for cleansing and clearing your emotional body knowing that water is a cleanser and helps to clear the emotional body. Use your shower time, brushing your teeth, watching your face as time to consciously feel yourself cleansing any negative emotions stuck from the previous day reflected back to you, as negative thoughts or emotions. Thank the element of water for its' blessings of support.

5.At some point after this, hopefully you are going to go fix yourself some breakfast. I encourage everyone to get their body system into a more pH balance by putting alkaline food or drink into their body first thing. Make a green power drink comprised of several organic vegetables, a few anti-oxidant power fruits and anti-inflammatory spices. Make that the first thing you put in your body versus anything acidic like coffee or eggs, toast or cereals. If you don't drink your drink until later in the morning then have a warm glass of lemon water to alkaline your body. As you are preparing yours and or others healthy break-fast, be mindful and centered and put your LOVE into the food and drink, raising its' frequency. Give thanks to Mother Earth and all Nature beings and elementals for the gifts of water, soil and air. Thank those that brought you your food from planting to delivery. Bless the Source from whom all things come.

6. Before leaving to go out into the outer world, take at least 15 minutes to sit outside and let the healing sunlight come onto your skin, even if it is cool outside, wear a coat and sit in the southern exposure away from any wind. Start a contemplation process while you gaze at the sky, clouds and sun and do this until you feel yourself sitting in pure presence. Leave an offering to Mother Earth and her nature kingdom for their blessings and support. I also have an inside prayer room for severe outdoor inclement days so that I can always give thanks, honor and send love and appreciation to Source, enlightened teachers, family/Ancestors, fellow cosmic and earth realm brothers and sisters and Nature for supporting and helping me to navigate my life and grow.

THE DAY ROUTINE

A SAMPLE OF THREE WAYS TO STAY IN PERSONAL SACRED SPACE THROUGHOUT YOUR COMMUNITY/ WORK DAY

1. The next trio of practices involves the middle of your day. As you try to stay mindful and present as much as you can throughout your day, free of all of the negative emotional mental activity that destroys our health and unbalances us, try to refocus on pure presence through increased self-awareness and more mindfulness. If you find yourself rushing around, recognize you're out of the present moment and stop and slow down.... bring your body into physical presence by moving more slowly through your activities and actions. If you find your mind running in loops recognize you're out of the present moment and stop it, just stop the thoughts and bring yourself back to the pure presence of the moment. If you're emotionally irritated, it's a sign that you're out of your present moment. Whether you're in the midst of working in your job, taking care of your children, engaging in your volunteer activities, cleaning your house. things will occur that will bring you out of the present moment. There are other tools to help you reset into presence, balance and positivity if increased self-awareness is not enough to shift things.

2. Should you feel yourself physically uncomfortable or in pain, stop and take a moment to do some tapping. Use EFT (Emotional Freedom Technique) to disburse your pain and reset yourself physically. If you find yourself getting emotionally upset, worried anxious, start to snap yourself back into presence by taking a moment to move out of reactivity into responding. Pair the snapping of your fingers with your breathe to create further awareness that you're in reactivity... Snap and then breathe deeply until you're back to a responding perspective going forward.

3. If you find yourself no longer in the present moment and dwelling on past and future activities, take a moment and walk about outside if you can and ground yourself by connecting with nature consciously and with intent focusing, with your feet on the ground and your mind on the sky or a tree or the beauty

around you in whatever form it exists. If you're inside and can't get outside make sure both feet are on the ground, just close your eyes and do some deep breathing exercises breathing in spiritual light from the creator and the universe into your body breathing out anything that doesn't serve by conscious intent and sending it into the earth. Ground yourself back into the present moment again and there you'll be connected balanced and energized.

THE EVENING ROUTINE

When you get home, there are 3 quick techniques to use to adjust from the outer world day and reset your field for the evening into a positive, balanced energized sacred field.

1.If you need to change your clothes after work go into your bedroom change your clothes and lay down on the bed for five minutes and take a power nap ...if you've got your kids around you or your dogs or cats around you cuddle together get some good oxytocin flowing between you and relax deeply. This is time to release from the days stress and to let your body get fully relaxed for about 5 to 10 minutes or as long as you want and have the time for. If you relax deeply enough you should begin to feel the flow of JOY...stay there for a bit and ENJOY it!!!

2.Once you get up, you will want to do some movement exercises because you want to release any stress that's left in the body and ultimately reset it for energy for the rest of the evening. Begin some movement exercise whether it is walking contemplatively, walking with your dog, going for a run or a stent at the gym. The goal here is to do what you do in movement consciously as a disconnection from the day to release it. Make a conscious connection to the earth releasing out the days' events and experiences, feeling fully the joy of the healing energies of nature with each step coming into your awareness and energy field, filling the void. Stay focused as much as you can in the present moment and consciously stop negative thoughts and release emotions without judgment as they come up.

3. At the end of that movement activity you will want to do a final exercise where you get consciously connected directly to the earth for spiritual rejuvenation and healing ...so when you're done, stay outside and sit in a chair with your feet on the ground with your shoes off. Ideally sit on the ground or lay on the ground for 15 minutes by the sea or under a tree. Have your space designated previously and have your movement activity end there. Take 15 minutes to get connected fully with the earth rejuvenated by the healing energies from the forest or the water, sand, grass or trees. You are naturally receiving the highest form of healing energy on the planet in nature created for us for this purpose by the Divine/ Source /Creator/Great Spirit/ God. Take it into your body, mind and heart most fully with your presence and intention to receive healing and to re-balance into your sacred self. From that space you will continually help your body and mind set up new habits aligned with health happiness and harmony.

It is good to create your own daily sacred healing rituals and routines so that you can receive the benefits of energy, clarity, peace, balance and joy in your life every day. From that place of solitude, simplicity, surrender, presence, sharing, joy, gratitude and divine connection comes sacred awareness and living!

WEEKLY SACRED LIVING
LIFESTYLE PRACTICES
(What are yours? Here are mine!)

I remember in my early work years when I moved out to the Pacific Northwest, I was shocked, coming from the East Coast, at the work ethic which was really work to play. Having come from a place where work was all there was and you played only if you had time leftover my staff called me the wicked witch of the East...I didn't appreciate the Seattle play perspective back then but by the time I was 40 and living back on the East Coast, I was well into stress health problems but also starting to get the understanding and value of creating a balanced life in order to live a long and healthy time. I began to establish sacred daily routines and weekly routine's that changed my mental, emotional and physical health greatly. I left my 7-7 job and went rogue into a new profession that allowed me to create a weekly lifestyle that would support my newly developed life affirming joy filled sacred practices. These sacred practices have helped me to reset my energetic field during several times of crisis in my life subsequently, as life challenges continue to go on. But as I have continued to engage in day-to-day sacred life practices I now, at age 60 feel more vibrant, alive and healthier than at any time previously in my life.

I have a weekly regime that I still try and stick to as often as I can to keep my week in balance. My ratio is for every 2-3 days of work there should be a day of play which can look like doing things that you enjoy or doing things that you do that aren't work related in a joyful way. I currently do volunteer work three days a week at the animal shelter and I visit elderly family members one day a week. I also have a day where I need to do my house cleaning and cooking and shopping so I really have five days of work like the average person.

On work days......What I have done that has been a game changer in my life is to commit those days to focus on sharing my gifts in pure presence. I use my daily sacred regimes to set myself up to stay in pure presence as much as possible while I'm at my workplace while also staying mindfully aware of my talents and gifts and claiming my abilities while doing my work. Each situation that comes in front of me is an opportunity to practice being authentic and present with any person I am interacting within any decision I am making or message I am sending. In this place I send truth and love out around me whatever the content. When I use the days experience as a reflection of my gifts and an opportunity to practice presence it makes the day go quicker, smoother, easier and feels more purpose filled.

On chore days....My two days of chores and personal responsibilities are spent in the spirit of surrender and simplicity. I don't rush my way through any of it and I stay in the moment of each activity with the intent to keep my moment simple and experience one thing at a time. I surrender my focus and my efforts when listening to others I talk with. As people cross my path I endeavor to see everyone around me as a spark of creation to be cared for, understood and cultivated.

On play days....I commit my other two free days to play, consciously sitting in joy and playing in my spiritual connection to everything and everyone around me. I spend my Sundays, after my spiritual communion in the morning in nature, as many do in church, playing outdoors in the sunlight in nature in the fresh air. I move a lot, I ride a bike for a little bit, I walk on the beach and if I can, go swimming and shell picking. I use Sunday for that as it's a great day energetically to play as most everyone around me is in that mode and it really supports your own decisions to do that energetically. I choose another day off in the middle of the week to play and that helps balance the week out. If you can take 2 days off to play a week DO IT!! A sacred life does involve a complete day of rest at least once a week and in this stressful world I'm a proponent of two days. We should only be working four days a week at our jobs in modern times because we need to keep in balance the stress of our modern lifestyles with regenerating play time. We also know through extensive research that we are more productive the other 4 when we do this. If you still work a 5/day week, try to work from home some days or make a play date with yourself for at least an hour before or after work days.

"Well-designed and maintained green spaces in cities such as parks, community gardens and tree lined streets lower the rate of violent crimes, make communities safer and keep people healthier."
-CORNELL UNIVERSITY RESEARCH PROJECT

One of the things I have consciously chosen to do throughout my life is to live in places where there is a lot of nature around me so I can access it easily and quickly as part of a daily routine for my own ongoing healing and happiness. If you live in a city and you don't have a lot of nature immediately around you, you always have parks and parks are there for this purpose ....so access your local, state and conservation parks if you don't have a yard or green neighborhood and get out there, because nature is the greatest healing remedy on the planet and God given to humans to keep us in right relationship with ourselves and to help us stay on the sacred path.

In Closing...

As I start and end every day in a sacred way, I always offer a resonant sacred mantra and prayer into the Universal field of ONENESS and, because of the Universal Law, as above so below, I believe and know, that it is already so… DO NOT forget the power that you are as a spark of Source energy. Everything that you do, say, think and feel is imbued with powerful Source manifestation energy and unlimited creative potential. You are connected to and affecting everyone and everything. Now, see, act and speak from this place of powerful DIVINE knowing and begin to change your world and the world, one Divine vision at a time.

MY SACRED MANTRAS

I AM A CHILD OF THE UNIVERSE. I AM CONNECTED TO EVERYONE AND EVERYTHING IN THIS VAST COSMOS OF SOURCE CREATION.

WHATEVER I DO AFFECTS THE ALL.

MY MISSION IS LOVE. THERE IS ONLY LOVE AND THE AWARENESS, CREATING AND EXPERIENCE OF ALL OF THE MANY FORMS OF LOVE OR THE LACK THEREOF.

I CHOOSE TO CREATE AS LOVE TODAY AND EVERYDAY, ENVISIONING AND CALLING FORTH PEACE, ABUNDANCE, HEALTH, SAFETY, FREEDOM AND HAPPINESS FOR MYSELF AND ALL BEINGS ON THIS PLANET AS MY LIVING EXPERIENCE OF LIFE.

SACRED LIVING IS MY EARTH BASED REALITY, ...AND SO IT IS!!!!

A Visionary Prayer for
Daily Sacred Living

I see a beautiful day ahead of me. All of us are
helping and caring for each other.

Things get done easily and effortlessly
in the FLOW of Divine right timing.

Everyone is aware of what they need to do to learn and grow
spiritually and take responsibility for their choices and actions.

We all show the utmost respect for ourselves, others, our
planet Earth, all the creatures, sentient beings
and substances in and on it and throughout our Universe.

We are all prospering in good health,
happiness and financial abundance together.

There is peace, freedom, equality and justice in the world.

We create endlessly, expansively and joyously
with light and love as our paint brush.

We all sense our connection to each other and delight in
our unity, our love for each other, all sentient beings, our
Mother Earth, the Universe and our Source of ALL THAT IS.

We know ourselves as infinite Divine Light and Love and in that
knowing, we merge with the Source and become the ONENESS of it all.

Each of our days are filled with the JOY of this Divine love experience
and we always remember that: WE ARE DIVINE, WE ARE LIGHT, WE
ARE PEACE, WE ARE ABUNDANCE, WE ARE LOVE... and so it is!!!

SECTION III

A Call to Sacred Living-
THE COMMUNITY JOURNEY

"Sacred Living Solution Circles"
GUIDEBOOK
-Rationale
-Process Explanations
-Facilitator's Guide
-Participant Agenda and Guidelines

SACREDLY LIVING IN COMMUNITY

RATIONALE

Why do we need to engage in more sacred ways of living and being in our families, neighborhoods, political groups, schools, social gatherings, workplaces, businesses, government and communities? Why do we need sacred living values, principles and solutions in play in community arenas at this time on planet Earth?

"... to dream a world into being where our children can live in peace,
where nature thrives, and where the rivers and the air are clean"
"... it is happening now. Now is the time to choose."
-INTERPRETATIONS OF INKA, Q'ERO PROPHESIES

With our personal and collective over focus on our human material world realities, there is constant stress and producing great challenges and causing limitations for so many people on the planet. People are living in more distrust and disconnection, separation and scarcity thinking and behavior. Our balanced, trusting, sacred nature has been subsumed and forgotten. When we live life without a sacred lens or purpose, we do not remember that we are all connected, entangled and are affecting each other by our every thought. We lose respect for others unlike ourselves and reverence for the planet as a conscious sentient being. We stop becoming responsible for our outer and inner resources, personal and collective decisions and individual and institutional power. As a result, we are unable to create and lead fully inspired sacred communities, holistically driven, where everyone thrives. We need to journey back to find our sacred way individually and collectively for the health, happiness and harmony of ourselves, our communities, our earth and the world.....But where do we start?

THE PATH OF PEACE

Start with the known.
A place out of harmony. Lacking vitality.
In conflict with the ideal.
A swamp of stagnant thought.

Move through to the unknown.
Seeing a possibility.
The belief that it can be otherwise.
The idea of reclamation.

Set your intention.
Create a path.
Every step a leap of faith.
Unknown, but moving you towards your goal.

Begin immediately and patiently.
Build a foundation growth to start.
Find your center. The point of balance.
Stake it with your intentions.

Make fertile what was once fallow.
Rebuild soils that will hold tender new roots.
Volunteers, plant and human, working side by side.
Together nurture the seedlings of a different future.

The CIRCLE of Life grows.
Native plants nourished by
Sacred Native gifts.
Prayers for healing placed deep in the Earth.
The CIRCLE of Peace grows.
Surprised by its own unfolding.

Rippling outwards to embrace the children.
Helping them blossom as they call in a New Earth.

A SACRED SPACE to rest, listen and respond.
No place for self-imposed ideas.
Only room to co-create heartfelt outcomes.
The result is unknown, but the path is clear!

Contemplate a new integrity.
Dream a new harmony in the land.
Follow the path to a place where you can
Live a growing song of Peace.

- Annie and Elvin Hess, Sept. 2009

This exquisite piece was written over 10 years ago by dear friends of mine, who at the time, were directors of a healing retreat center in Virginia. Their words and call to sacred action have never been more relevant then today. That sacred healing and teaching center brought people from the community together to commune, share ideas and empower each community member to holistically take action to improve their personal and collective world, the earth and all beings on it. Being part of this community for several years myself, I was supported and supportive of others in reclaiming and continuously evolving a sacred path for each member of the community during and after our gatherings. We embraced collaboration, cooperation and co creation as sacred tenants of change-making.

"Humans are driven by connection and the need for care...We share common humanity by design;"
- THE CHARTER FOR COMPASSION

I have been holding sacred community space for over 30 years for people in my communities wherever I have lived. I found it an essential tool for my own spiritual growth and development of my sacred nature, as did those who attended. Some of my groups were based around spiritual practices to further personal growth and education...some were large sacred circles, some small. I, at one time even owned and operated an interfaith spiritual retreat center in St Croix USVI which was open to all island residents and any visitors to the island. It was a place where we shared in sacred communion, ceremonies, education and support of one another. After I sold the business I found that we could meet in homes and small centers around the island just as effectively but, that it was essential, that we meet regularly, stay open minded, encourage and embrace everyone in the community, listen respectfully and deeply to one another and support each other in action out in the community. This is a sacred way of being in right relationship with one another.

Fast forward to 2020, A Call to Sacred Living year, when the world began to reflect back to us the lack of sacredness in our daily lives but also began to allow us to begin the possibility of resetting ourselves sacredly as a result. As was mentioned in the first part of this book, sacred living, the personal journey has many paths and facets... in prolonged solitude we begin to see with new eyes and value things differently...simplicity becomes valued and easier to attain then we thought making our lives more effortless...when we are made to surrender our rat race agendas we begin to see that our lives are not always serving to keep us healthy and peaceful....without many tasks to DO we begin to experience staying more mindful in the moment and we are more serene and present and able to listen to each other and our inner voice more fully...leaving our JOBS temporarily or permanently, we are better able to begin to sense and get back in touch with our true nature and our authentic desires and purpose... sharing our gifts begins to be meaningful and necessary...our time spent with our families and friends are no longer to be taken for granted and we embrace them even more fully for the JOY that they bring us....that walk to the beach which is part of our exercise regime every morning becomes revered for its healing, uplifting communion with nature....remembering ourselves again as members of the human race by seeing that the impact of our life choices directly affect each other profoundly, makes us more caring and compassionate....community gatherings are seen as important and necessary for the special feelings only gotten when in direct contact with each other….and in many cases as we begin to experience ourselves as more entangled with one another and our planet and all beings on it, we maybe even recognize ourselves as part of a much larger existence. 2020 was our wake-up "Call to Sacred Living", a clarion call to begin to see the importance of learning the many ways back to becoming a sacred, heart-centered individual and community.

> *"The EARTH will settle when the hearts of mankind settle"*
> **-NO EYES**

This "settling" is just beginning to emerge in the hearts and minds of only a portion of earth travelers. At present on the planet we are still living in extreme times and most people only awaken to their sacred nature, growing and changing, in response to extreme circumstances and the pain body. Trauma and tragedy still often informs our thoughts and colors the lens of our decisions and choices.

Modern societal expectations have put constant pressure on families and communities to focus on the material world versus the sacred world. Often people spend all their time on work and material acquisition just to survive. When people are in survival, they are stressed and there is an under focus on inner development and nurturing relationships, community and citizenship participation, the absence of which can create separation, strain and stress in the home, community and state.

> *In western societies, "We live in a toxic, overly*
> *materialistic society...with great amounts of social isolation*
> *and subsequent alienation from one another."*
> **-DR GABOR MATE', MD "(TRAUMA SPECIALIST)**

So, if adults are stressed and often without sacred vision, unable to offer sacred guidance, then children experience and feel this as lack of attentiveness, lack of family time, lack of nurturing support, peers raising children rather than parents. Social isolation and addiction are rampant. Bullying and outing people when expressing their uniqueness is cutting the lifeblood from the wellspring of individual genius and talents of our community. Violent behavior in all its forms, as the furthest expression of sacred disconnection has created further problems...alienation, division, addiction, suicide, aggression, hatred and greed toward one another is rampant in our world.

This does not need to be!! We are wired for empathy, connection, love and compassion as our true nature. It's past time for us to get back to our true nature... our sacred nature...but how?

"Never doubt that a small group of thoughtful, committed citizens can change the world. It's the only thing that ever has"
-MARGARET MEADE

As a young college student studying international relations in the late 70's I had the great privilege of sitting with Margaret Meade in a forum discussing the challenges and wonders of third world societies and the many ways to understand the dynamics of those regions. As she described their problems surviving in an emerging modern world, she shared some of their solutions that were grass roots focused and inspiring in their connection and respect for each member in their community and very sacred in nature, despite the numerous difficulties and hurdles they faced to create change.

Intrigued about their community sacred practices, I began traveling to third world countries to explore those cultures first hand. As I explored their social, emotional and cultural dynamics, I encountered communities with lots of material world problems, with little wealth, but with lots of spiritual wisdom. Some communities had limited resources but had learned to harness all their needs with minimal impact on the earth. Most cultures were communally driven and had enormous respect for their elders compared to modern cultures. Compassion and comradery were the way most work got done. The group need was considered as important as the individual needs. People were happy and interconnected and supported each other despite the material world challenges. I admired them for their sacred qualities and nature as they were always showing the utmost respect and appreciation for each other and the Planet. These were not 'primitive' people at all. In fact these people were wise and really quite evolved.

I concurrently, became disillusioned once home with American/Western communities who were and are very overly individualism oriented, consumption and materially driven. As the years went on though, I saw that when some of these third world societies were given the opportunity to enter the modern world, that their materially driven lifestyle went up and their sacred living went down. Instead of using local ingenuity, sacred practices and community strength, people used money to solve problems like their western neighbors. Days were spent working to buy things, debt was incurred and self-sovereignty was lost. They became detached from nature and their ability to feed and heal themselves was diminished as their major efforts and time were focused on their jobs and paying their bills, sadly the demise of most of the current modern world.

In my later years, when traveling around the world in search of the sacred, I began to refocus my visits on personal sacred experiences with people living in the towns I was visiting. Each persons' story, was experienced as a gift by me when listening deeply to the journey of another whose lifestyle was so extremely different than mine. As we shared our life stories, I came to see and appreciate what they uniquely brought to the table and together we discovered the areas between us of common ground. What developed in me was deep compassion and reverence for each persons' individual life journey, whether it was similar to mine or not. My sacred lens was developing through my experience of shared humanity as well as our mutual appreciation of our differences. Over time a deep bond developed with a perfect stranger from another part of the world. We were in what the indigenous would call, sacred communion.

My newly developed sacred lens would soon become a very valuable overlay to the process that I was using in my community work back home in schools, workplaces, community groups as an organizational consultant. I had decided that I was going to facilitate organization strategic planning in a more sacred way. If the basis of all sacred community was the ongoing cultivation and demonstration of mutual respect, reverence and regard of its members, it would be essential in the beginning of my new, more sacred process, to facilitate bringing people into deeper relationship with one another in order to create a better understanding and develop compassionate regard for each other as a sacred foundation. From this place each person would be able to listen more deeply to one another and then common ground could be discovered that would create the bridge between everyone. In a state of sacred communion, group collaboration would ideally occur more easily as the organization worked toward consensus building, solving their challenges and creating sacred solutions.

The final step would be to assist every individual at the workplace to uncover and learn how to utilize their talents, experiences and passion so as to become an effective sacred team member when implementing the new solution plan. When seen, listened to and honored for their individual contributions, each member in the group would feel more empowered and become a more capable active participant and leader in the group solution execution process.

What I had done without realizing it, was to return to many of the sacred ways of the indigenous cultures that I had visited in my early years traveling abroad. I had created a model for sacred community problem solving and living for organizations and businesses in the modern world.

One of the best ways for anyone to start to create sacred community within a group, involves the development of a nurturing sacred empowerment circle designed to entrain each person in the teachings and expressions of sacred values, principles and practices. Over my many years as both a sacred spiritual leader and community organizational consultant I have learned how to merge the sacred into the western community process. The model I now use is a body of work that I call, "sacred living solution circles". It is designed to do just that, facilitate compassionate circular leadership for group/ community problem solving based in sacred values, principles and practices.

A sacred, values driven community is more likely to take care of all of its people which provides, in kind, for the thriving and safekeeping of the community at large, the people, services, government and businesses. When a sacred community is consciously living the reality of its Cosmic spiritual nature, with full knowing that we are ALL energetically entangled, connected, and that whatever affects one affects ALL, amazing things will be able to be accomplished! Quantum entanglement has now been proven as reality in the emerging science of quantum physics… it's not just a secret of indigenous, eastern and ancient traditions any more. "Quantum entanglement occurs when 2 particles (people) become inextricably linked and whatever happens to one immediately affects the other regardless of how far apart, they are." This phenomenon was first observed by Albert Einstein and at the time he labeled it" spooky action at a distance". Now imagine when multiple communities entangled with each other with full spiritual awareness can intentionally manifest as sacred action out in the world!!!

The indigenous people of our Planet have always known and never forgotten that everything is living energy and that we are all connected and entangled and affect each other all of the time. All of us are, Divine and deserving to be cared for and about. Each humans' gifts are to be valued and utilized. Everyone is expected to give and take, contribute and reap the benefits from the work of the whole community. Living life in harmony, respect and balance within ourselves, with others and with nature, not separate, is a given, for WE are ALL one!

So, when we send peace from our hearts to anyone it is felt all over the world, when a bird sings it opens a flower, when we help another, we are helping everyone, when we pray for another to be healed, we heal ourselves. This is the nature of a loving sacred connected Universe and the truth of our sacred reality and power. When we use sacred practices in our own lives, with others and in our group gatherings, we will amplify exponentially the individual and community intentions and effects. What better reason to develop and turn on our sacred super powers and join together to bring peace, love, prosperity, joy and health to ourselves and our communities.

**We are that small group of thoughtful,
committed citizens that can change the world!!!**

Implementing a "Sacred Living Solutions Circles" model as a template for learning how to generate sacred action is the first step towards creating sacred community life.

PROCESS EXPLANATIONS

Below is a model for executing a "sacred living solution circle" within a community or group gathering. By teaching and supporting individuals within the group to learn to execute the sacred ways of compassionate collaboration based around 4 cornerstone sacred principles, 7 sacred personal values and 4 sacred guiding precepts, the group will then have the tools and skills needed to bond and build a community with effective sacred group communicating, relating and decision making. When you create a culture based in compassion and mutual respect, you can develop sacred solutions to the community's challenges, and facilitate community harmony.

"Sacred Living Solution Circles"
Empowerment Gatherings for families, groups, communities on the path to sacred living

To start a sacred living solution circle in your community or group, albeit a family, social group, township, neighborhood, work place or school, it requires consciously choosing to come together regularly with sacred focus and intent. A sacred process is facilitated by a trained sacred living solutions facilitator until the community, in week 3, takes over the facilitation process after 2 weeks of on the ground training with the facilitator.

The circle gathering takes place outdoors in a Nature setting whenever possible, so that the connection to Mother Earth can be felt, experienced and garnered to further develop and support sacred growth. All activities are conducted in a circle seating arrangement and everyone is encouraged and expected to participate throughout the gathering in equal proportion of time.

As the group engages in sacred ways you will begin to see people in the group become more connected and compassionate toward one another. From a place of community connection, common ground can be established and collaboration and consensus building can take place more easily, creating the platform for sacred solutions to arise, as the community evolves into a new, more sacred form. The following are the steps to creating your own sacred living solutions circle.

STEP #1

I do believe that the first step for each person within the sacred circle is to begin to commit to cultivating a personal individual sacred living lifestyle at home so that they can more easily and effectively assist in the creation of a sacred community. The first part of this book has been devoted to the understanding of the need and the tools and practices to cultivate the behaviors and beliefs on a path to individual sacred living. The book will be available to any participant in the group upon request. There are also opportunities for individuals to develop some sacred living lifestyle skills throughout the sacred living solutions circle group process as well.

STEP #2

The group collectively needs to ascribe to sacred core principles, values and sacred behavior practices with the understanding that we are all entangled and connected to each other. Direction for this can be found within the ancient wisdom teachings, modern sacred teachings and religious texts. I derived the majority of the underpinning of this body of work from visiting, studying, experiencing and living in sacred communities from various religions, native traditions and walks of life in an effort to understand what sacred living is, why it is important and how to develop and sustain it in one's life for the betterment of self, the community and the planet. This is what was revealed to me and is incorporated into this "Sacred Living Solution Circles" work as foundational principles, values and precepts for sacred action.

The 4 Sacred Principles from universal laws and ancient wisdom teachings:

These principles are the basis of many sacred indigenous cultures, created for keeping the people in Divine spiritual "right" relationship with themselves, each other, their community, Mother Earth, and the Creator; in order to maintain harmony and balance in the world!

Remembering Universal Truths
- We are part of a great Cosmic creation of consciousness, love and light
- We are beings of living energy and light that vibrate at a frequency
- We are energetic spiritual beings having a human experience
- We are all energetically entangled and connected to each other and what we do to ourselves we do to each other
- We create the reality we live in with our beliefs, thoughts and feelings
- We are all unique creations from the Source and all have a unique contribution to offer the world
- We live in a universe that is designed to give us whatever we ask for with our hearts desire all of the time

Respecting everyone and everything
- We must learn to listen deeply to truly hear and come to understand and care about another persons' inner truths and desires.
- We must learn the art of allowing and accepting that each person has their own important journey to take and not judge others paths. Until we have walked in another's moccasins...
- We must recognize the importance of encouraging the use and expression of talents, abilities, gifts and messages of each person as an essential part of the process of creating balance and solutions for the greater good.
- We must acknowledge that the earth and all sentiment beings are our partners in this experience of expanding and expressing ourselves on this planet and we must take care of them all as well as ourselves to survive and to thrive.

Responsibility for our actions

- Choice is our greatest power... we always have free will to think, feel, speak and believe whatever we wish.
- It is critical to shift our beliefs, thoughts, emotions and actions from victim-hood; fear, blame and judgment to empowered; self-aware, self-realized and personal responsibility for our actions, thoughts and emotions and what they create.
- We need to live in the present moment so as to fully embrace and experience precious moment to moment life and not create from past problems or future worries.
- It is imperative to move ourselves from reaction to responding by pausing our reactive thoughts and emotions to an experience and allow our intuitive self to observe and respond from a higher perspective, so that we get higher answers and experiences.
- We must seek balance in body, mind and heart in order to bring peace and balance to oneself, the planet and the world.

Reverence for all life

- Honor the Divine, God/Goddess/Goodness in everything.
- See through the eyes of the childlike soul self.
- Celebrate the beauty, wonder, gifts and blessings of Creation...nature, the planet and the cosmos.
- Give thanks and focus on what is working in your life, what you have, just give thanks for it all, as everyone and everything is a lesson and opportunity to learn, to grow and love more.
- Give an offering of your appreciation whenever you take anything as you must give something back in return, it's the Law of Sacred Reciprocity and maintains balance in the world.

"Certain Universal values help us flower"

-CHARTER FOR COMPASSION

The 7 sacred personal values below are necessary to be embraced and imbued by each participant in order to build, execute and maintain a community sacred living circle. Applying these values in our daily life will allow us to more readily and easily treat each other with respect, reverence and to take responsibility for the effects of our words and actions toward ourselves and one another.

Flexibility, Patience, Humility, Honesty, Open Mind, Gratitude, Kindness

Flexibility

1. Learn to be flexible when interacting with one another
   - Be willing to shift and change position for a moment and suspend personal thoughts and beliefs
   - Bend when feeling rigid and seek an easy and effortless stance
   - Be adaptable to see and use new options, patterns and build capabilities

Patience

2. Patiently take the time to listen deeply to one another
   - Listen more, talk less
   - Don't react when listening to others speak or act...pause and breathe
   - Respond in a careful and thought filled way

Humility

3. Choose to surrender your ego and share from a place of the humble heart
   - Act unpretentiously not boastfully and speak calmly, from your true, centered self, from your heart
   - Be willing to surrender your need to control others or the situation at hand
   - Put others on equal ground with yourself seeing their ideas, thoughts and feelings equally important to yours

Honesty

4. Be willing to look at and own your thoughts, feelings and choices
   - Live by the truths of Universal Laws
   - Do not deceive or lie to yourself or others
   - Do not take anything away from another

Open Mind

5. Stay open minded when listening to others opinions and thoughts
   - Allow others to take a path that is different from your own and see it as one that is valuable
   - Accept that others have their own journeys to take without judging them as good or bad, right or wrong
   - Adopt a supportive nature to empower yourself and others to learn, grow and evolve without attachment

Gratitude

6. Give thanks for your gifts, blessings and opportunities and be appreciative to others in celebration
   - Feel joyful when experiencing what is positive and good in your life and others' lives
   - Express thanks for assistance and teachings from others
   - Claim a positive, optimistic, solutions outlook on life and share it with others

Kindness

7. Demonstrate kindness to others through regular acts of compassion, forgiveness and generosity
   - Be generous in sharing your time and things with others without expecting anything in return
   - Consider others feeling as equally important to your own
   - If you feel slighted or wronged, forgive the person for being human, if not the deed, if it has caused harm, pain or suffering to you or another

The 4 guiding precepts of sacred living solution setting:

The following guiding precepts MUST be acknowledged AND included in any final sacred solution plan that the community develops. In order for it to be a sacred solution arising from our spiritual nature, it must reflect the quantum truth that we are all connected to each other. All of the great religious traditions and spiritual wisdom councils have core precepts by which their communities operate and they are non-negotiable.

I. DO NO HARM

"If you can, help others; if you cannot do that, at least do not harm them"
- THE DALAI LAMA

II. CULTIVATE UNCONDITIONAL LOVE FOR ONE ANOTHER

"Radica l(Divine) love is channeled through humanity. It has to be lived and embodied, shared and refined, not in the heavens but right here and now in the messiness of earthly life"
- SAFI (A SUFI TEACHER)

III. ENSURE PLANETARY CARE AND SUSTAINABILITY FOR 7 GENERATIONS

"Look and listen for the welfare of the whole people and have always in view not only the present, but also the coming generations."
- CONSTITUTION OF THE IROQUOIS NATION

IV. UPHOLD THE CARE OF THE GREATER GOOD FOR THOSE WHO ARE DEPENDENT

"The measure of a civilization is how it treats its weakest members"
-GANDHI

Each final solution must integrate these 4 sacred precepts in order to be approved for implementation by a Sacred Living Solutions community.

SACRED LIVING SOLUTIONS COMMUNITIES
Our Vision and Mission...

To make the world a more sacred place; loving, unified, safe, prosperous, healthy and sustainable for all beings on it! When gathering and actioning in local communities; if we embrace and respect our unique differences, support and encourage each other to share our individual purpose and passion while also requiring personal responsibility from each individual for their actions and behavior, then our communities will more easily unify and together be able to seek and find common ground, allowing for sacred solutions to the community's problems and challenges to be expressed. When we remember that we each are infinite spirits in creative human bodies, all of us connected while living in this Earth experience together; then when any community participant grows sacredly it helps all community participants to become more sacred. When a community grows sacredly it supports other communities to do the same. We commit to this vision and mission for ourselves and for the world.

Our Plan...

To hold regular sacredly facilitated community gatherings in any community interested in this mission. Meetings are to be held ideally in a public outdoor space at, a school, organization, business or personal home depending on the community type. Everyone from all walks of life having anything to do with that community are invited and encouraged to attend and participate in sharing their dreams, gifts and solutions to the community challenges. As the community gathers together in deeper connection and support for one another, there will develop a greater sense of tolerance and belonging for each person in the community. During the process of community bonding and building, the community will seek to create a vision and plan for sacred solutions to the community's or group's chosen challenges and problems to solve. This will occur using a facilitated process that is engaged throughout in a sacred manner so that people can learn, practice and grow their own sacred living skills and values. Ultimately, the people in the community will become more collaborative, work from a place of comradery and compassion, and be more effective and cooperative when solving challenges and implementing solutions for the community to thrive together ongoing.

Our Goals...

Goal #1

To support individuals within the community with their emotional and spiritual growth and sacred understanding by offering training in sacred living practices that facilitate personal empowerment during the process.

"In healing yourself you become a healer of others, you are healing the planet...there is no more sacred work than this....when you are in right relationship with yourself you are fulfilling your sacred mission"
- NATIVE AMERICAN ELDER

Sacred community living first involves becoming an awake, aware and healed observer of the truth of your own life This allows you to be better able to live as the realization of your authentic self, responsibly responding, not reacting to your experiences. By equipping yourself with healing tools to release dis-empowering victim patterns, choosing instead to express through your authentic self as divine love, joy, respect, gratitude and peace out into the world and with others, you begin to intentionally live on purpose. That is one of the most important things you can do for yourself, your family, your community and the planet.... When you express, share and use your gifts you expand your light and you inspire others to do the same!

"Do you choose to share your suffering or your wisdom?"
- CAROLINE MYSS

CONTEMPLATION -HEALING- PERSONAL RESPONSIBILITY

Goal #2

To assist people to develop greater compassion for each other through relationship bonding and building within the community problem solving process. Compassionate loving kindness expressed, moves us closer toward living as the sacred truth that we are, ALL ONE (E Pluribus Unum). It allows us to work together as a community in greater unity and harmony.

> *".... in a time of crisis, the peoples of the world*
> *must rush to get to know each other"*
> **- JOSE MARTI**

Relationship development is the first step in assisting groups of people across the divide of diversity, misunderstandings and differences ... personality, cultural, economic, religious, political and ethnic. By embracing each persons' unique path and deeply listening to each other's needs, desires, personal values and notions of what is important, we find common ground, develop respect and compassion for one another and offer a reverence for each persons' journey, as the basis for building a sacred community.

> *"We can improve our relationships with others by leaps and*
> *bounds if we become encouragers instead of critics."*
> **- JOYCE MEYER**

CONNECTION-RELATIONSHIP-APPRECIATION

Goal #3

To cultivate and realize a vision of a world that works for all where the compassionate sacred community works together in service to the greater good of the planet as well as itself. When all of the people in the community have greater ability to cultivate common ground awareness, collaborative capabilities and co-creative decision-making capacity then they can take these abilities out into the other areas of their lives and apply, assist and activate sacred action everywhere.

"The greatness of a community is most accurately measured
by the compassionate action of its members"
- CORETTA SCOTT KING

If the truth is that we are all connected energetically to one another and everything on the planet and in the universe, then everything each of us does affects the other. Every thought that we have, every emotion, every action affects the ALL. When we effort to create a world that includes and works for everyone, we take care of ourselves, our loved ones, our community and our planetary family. Imagine public, private and personal partnerships, grassroots organizations and corporations collaborating and responding to a community's visions/ plans, to meet their local needs and challenges....and that by design, that community simultaneously is also affecting and in service to the planetary family in which is resides.

"Ethical, (effective) behavior likewise entails attunement to and harmony
with the whole esoteric field in which the human community rests..."
-HARRY STAFFORD

COOPERATION- COLLABORATION- COMMON GROUND

Goal #4

To acknowledge and utilize the wisdom of the earth, the indigenous ones and the ancestors who understood sacred things and who have always promoted sustainable practices on our planet Earth as a sacred way of life.

> *"We know the traditional models of linear economic growth based on a 'make, take and dispose' model do not work. Not even in the short term. A circular economy promotes the continual use of resources so there is much less waste in what we consume and produce. If we are to reach greater circularity, we need to get deeper into local development contexts, look for different measures to tell the story and to demonstrate how to generate and regenerate growth."*
>
> **- THE ECONOMIST**

We cannot live on this planet without the earths' resources of clean and healthy food, water, air, healing plants and energy. The Earth is truly all of our home and exists to take care of us. If you want to stay healthy and happy, you need to protect and take care of your home that takes care of you and all the beings that coexist with you. It just makes sense to follow these sacred ways!

Life on planet Earth exists as an ecology and all systems are connected, interdependent and responsive to each other. No one and nothing can be left out of the discussion or the solution as a sacred right. We need to acknowledge this truth and celebrate this unity reality every day in issuances of gratitude, ceremony and prayer.

> *"... ceremony is not the only time you're supposed to carry yourself in a sacred way. It is supposed to remind you that you are sacred and to carry yourself that way every day ...as you walk on the sacred earth treat each step as a prayer"*
>
> **- BLACK ELK**

GRATITUDE- HONORING- CELEBRATION

This is a different way of gathering ... a sacred way; with a focus on our "deepest shared humanity". Through the exchange of life stories and by deeply listening to one another as to what is important and sacred to each of us, each person will be seen and heard in a space of respect, dignity and inclusion. The community then becomes a sacred place of belonging for each person who enters. A greater sense of self- worth arises in everyone and each participant contributes in a more empowered way. What is subsequently created and expressed outwardly by a community that honors each other, is a sacred collaborative working toward solving its' own challenges and developing change plans that include shared visions of a loving, peaceful, healthy, prosperous life for each member of the community and the planet... sacred living solutions!

> *"There is no power for change greater than a*
> *community discovering what it cares about."*
> **- MARGARET WHEATLEY**

If you want to facilitate a sacred living solution circle in your family, school, group, business, government or community; below is a facilitators guide to help you get there.

"SACRED LIVING SOLUTION CIRCLES" FACILITATORS GUIDE

A "Sacred Living Solutions Circles" gathering requires 4 hours of committed time once or twice a month for at least one-year. Meetings can be held weekly, twice a month or once a month minimally depending on the groups interest and needs. There must be a core group of participants choosing to hold the space for the broader group of participates during the development, training and implementation of a sacred living solution circle in the first 6 months. Designated facilitators will receive training initially on the "Sacred Living Solutions Circles" process before and during gatherings from a trained facilitator. After 3 sessions of observing, co-facilitating and monitoring, the group should be ready to facilitate its own gathering. There should be at least 3 designated facilitators for the overall meeting management.

Gatherings should be held in a nature setting that is connected to, within or nearby the community that is gathering so that all community members have easy access to the location. A local park setting outdoors around a place of cover for inclement weather is best. People are encouraged to provide transportation to those community members who may not have transportation to the consensus chosen location (ie public transportation users). Participants are asked to bring their own chairs to sit on.

Music is an important part of this sacred circle process and the facilitators need to bring the music and simple sound system for playing during the gathering. Name tags need to be procured as well as light snacks and drinks. A collection basket is encouraged to provide the cost coverage for these items.

Upon arrival, during the meet and greet, light snacks and drinks time, each participant should be given a name tag and handout of the agenda, which will be reviewed with attendees by the facilitator at the start of the meeting. This form includes space for personal notes and reflection on ones use of the 4 sacred community principles, the 7 sacred values and the 4 sacred guiding precepts employed throughout the meeting.

Before starting the meeting facilitators assure that chairs are arranged in a circle and assure that people are sitting next to different people at each gathering. They then start the formal process 15 minutes after the hour of assigned start time and begin to facilitate the "get to know each other" session for the next 25 minutes, timing each of the 6/ Q and A, for 2 minutes each person back and forth.

Next the group is asked to choose a topic for solution setting that day. Facilitator puts this on the board for later. Then the contemplation session takes place to get the attendees into a relaxed and creative problem- solving mindset for 15 minutes.

After this, the facilitator presents the community challenge for discussion and solving which begins a 4-phase solution setting process. Break out group activities need to have a leader, recorder and time keeper established before engaging in group dialogue and these roles need to be rotated among the group members at every step in the solution process. This is part of the circle leadership training for leaderless circles. This lasts for 1 hour and 45 minutes.

Participants will be asked throughout the gathering to continually assess themselves on their performance using the 7 sacred values guidelines while engaging in the group process. If conflict develops during the meeting at any time, the SACRED REBOOT practices are engaged by the facilitator that reinstate the 4 core sacred principles to the gathering which will reset the meeting into a more sacred space. The facilitator should also put up the sacred principles, values, and precepts to be reviewed by the group before beginning the solutions discussions segment of the gathering and eventually overlay and embed them in the final solutions plan.

Celebration closings are the final facilitated activity before everyone departs. This lasts for 30 minutes.

Total minimum time allotted for a sacred gathering: 3.5 hours.

"SACRED LIVING SOLUTIONS CIRCLES" FACILITATORS AGENDA

I. Meet and Greet - I hour

    A. Informal sharing of some light food and drink optional while people first come into the space. Everyone gets a name tag and puts a nick name that reflects one positive attribute they bring to the group gathering. After 15 minutes, everyone gets seated in a circle and pairs off with people they have not come in with. At each gathering people will sit next to a new and different group participant throughout the meeting.

    B. The facilitator shares the sacred vision, plan, goals, values, principles and precepts as the foundation of the "sacred living solution circles" model with the group for 15 minutes.

    C. Using relationship bonding practices, people in the circle keep rotating to sit next to a different person at each new session they attend. Facilitator pairs people off. This takes 30 minutes, 2 minutes a query, back and fourth. Each person in the pair poses one of the queries to the person next to them and they have 2 minutes to answer. Session over when pairs have asked and answered each other all 6 queries.

        1. Find one thing in common with the person asking you this question

        2. Tell about something/someone that you love most in your life and why

        3. Share your greatest fear in life

        4. Offer one positive thing that you like about the person in your pair

        5. State one thing that you are good at

        6. Say something you are grateful for in your life

II. Community Challenge Selection - 15 min

    The facilitator then picks a topic from the community challenges board that feels important to the group that day taking feedback suggestions from the group until one is chosen. The chosen topic is placed off to the side of the board until after the group engages in an inner calming and centering process to create unification and cohesion within the group so that they can ascertain a more sacred solution to their chosen community challenge.

COMMUNITY CHALLENGES LIST
...FROM GLOBAL TO LOCAL

Help your community grow into a sacred, sustainable self-sovereign sanctuary of prosperity, health, peace, compassion and safekeeping for all

- Clean water, soil, air
- A thriving ecosystem
- Environmental justice and protection/Earth Rights
- Affordable and available healthy food sources
- Affordable and available alternative and allopathic, low and high tech healthcare services from preventive to palliative
- Safe, available and affordable housing of all types
- Effective Education services at all levels...academic, tech and trade
- Justice practices that uphold equality, human and animal rights
- Fostering and creating community art, culture and play spaces and events
- Assuring protection for all faiths, genders, ages, cultures to practice lifestyle choices
- Creating effective, connected and compassionate community leadership and management
- Affordable, safe and effective community utility, transportation and maintenance services
- Responsible, efficient, transparent fiscal oversight services
- Effective, transparent, compassionate police, fire and emergency care services
- Effective, transparent, compassionate social services for elderly, disabled and disadvantaged(homeless) members
- Extensive and diverse economic/business opportunities at livable wage rates assuring wage rates are within a range commiserate with the community cost of living

III. Contemplation and Visioning – 20 min.

Contemplation time is next and is used to ground and center us individually into our intuitive, higher self, our right brain, using sacred living visualization practices before we start a group sacred solution process.

"We use contemplation/meditation/calming practices to put the group into a calm state so that we can act with greater clarity from our resilient zone"

-LIFE UNIVERSITY COMPASSIONATE INTEGRITY PROGRAM

I. Play some soft soothing music and let everyone get into a quiet, relaxed space - 15 min.

    A. Ask everyone to gently contemplate their day and release the thoughts that are not positive or are causing stress by breathing them out and choosing to release them and let them go on the out breathe.... do this for a minute or 2. Breathe in positive energy to fill your body. Breathe out stress.

    B. Facilitate a guided visual meditation of a sacred space at the beach Tell them to see themselves basking in the sun, feeling the wind in their hair, rubbing their toes in the sand, letting the water wash around them to help to heal and continue to relax them. Do this for another minute or 2. Next allow each person to open up their imagination to remember what is sacred in their life, valuable, full of grace, a blessing and tell them to sit in that space for 3-4 minutes

    C. From this space present the group with the community problems that they chose to address today and have them create a sacred solution by asking them to contemplate on it from this more sacred place within, for a few more minutes. Tell them to write down their final solution thoughts.

IV. Sacred Solutions Discussion Time - 1.5 hours

The community problem is discussed with sacred living solutions applied: Reminders to all of the tenants of sacred gatherings reviewed. Principles, Values and Precepts

    I. Begin the sacred solution process. Acknowledge every individuals' ideas and visions in the gathering as valuable by listing each of their sacred solutions to the problem which arose during the end of their contemplation exercise, taking only one solution from each person in the circle. 15 min.

    2. Find Common Ground. As a total group, identify the intersections/ themes/groupings and put all of the solutions in 4 categories based on common factors among the total solution options. Facilitator can appoint

a scribe and timer for this 30 minute activity. Pick four categories first and then put each solution under a category. Highlight that there are things that we have in common even with different ideas on ways to go about making change and solving problems.

3. Help the group create sacred living solutions through Consensus Building. Put the entire group (going every other person) into 2 small groups. CHOOSE A SUB GROUP FACILITATOR, SCRIBER AND TIMER. This will last 15 minutes. Have each group pick 1 solution among the 4 solutions using discussion and consensus decision making. Then each group presents back to the entire gathering their 1 solution for the community. There should be only 2 solution options now to choose from.

4. Next ask each of the 2 groups to attempt to create a solution that includes both groups ideas through Collaboration of ideas. This takes 15 minutes. Record the 2 final solutions on the board. Then have each person in both groups vote for what they think is the best solution and let the majority vote stand as the working solution for that meeting.

5. Begin a discussion around major objections from anyone in the group to the solution chosen and let each person state their objection uninterrupted. Allow anyone who wants to counter or explain in response to the objection to do so. Rework the solution if a majority vote feels that any piece of it should be changed and do this together from a place of compassionate regard for one another, for 10-15 minutes.

6. Sacred living solutions need to incorporate the following 4 guiding precepts of sacred solution setting: Put these on the board:15 min *do no harm, cultivate radical love, look out for the planet and seven generations, benefit the greater good and weakest members*

7. Review the majority final solution for alignment with the 4 guiding sacred precepts of sacred solution standards and recraft the solution using sacred language that uphold these precepts. Use this process to help coalesce and unify the group. This takes 20 minutes.

8. This is done with the entire group for 30 minutes. Develop a simple plan with the group to implement the solution strategy (what, how, where, who, when) so that anyone can choose to follow up, in their sphere of influence, in the execution of the final group sacred solution. Encourage

people to reach out to local community groups/agencies/organizations to collaborate with them in implementing the solution after the gathering ends.

V. Celebration and Closing - 15 min.

This is to be conducted while standing together in a closed circle...start with a silent moment to allow individuals to invoke their spiritual centering from their personal practice place. Use three deep breathes for release and relaxation to cohere and connect the group.

First... Anyone who wants to put someone in the circle for focused intent of healing does so and the group sends their love and positive energy to each other (sending love and light for the highest and most benevolent outcome)

Second... Anyone who wants to express something they celebrated this week or year in their life does so and the group shares in with their celebration energy (whistles, hoots and claps)

Third... Turn to each person next to you and give thanks to one another for participating together in the collective search for sacred living solutions to benefit the local community and or the planet (shaking hands and giving hugs)

Fourth... Play a closing song that is inspiring, uplifting to motivate the groups sacred efforts going forward together in the circle gatherings and out in the community by sharing in celebration energy (singing, dancing, moving)

CONFLICT RESOLUTION STRATEGIES

If or when conflict arises between or among the group at any point in time, there are three practices in conflict resolution to bring harmony back to the group.

It's called the SACRED REBOOT

Remember...Responsibility - The first practice for the facilitator to engage the group in, is an activity called the SNAP. The snap requires that everyone STOP the moment conflict arises and release from their thoughts, actions and words by literally snapping their fingers. It's an exercise for getting people to move from reactivity back into responding. Everyone snaps their fingers together for up to a minute or two and then stops when they "snap back into reality" as their responder self. Then they take three deep breaths, three deep in and out breaths to relax and center and bring themselves back to that place in the meditation where the body becomes harmonized within once again.

Remember...Respect - The next step is to restore respect among the group and that requires that the facilitator ask each person to turn to the person next to them and shake that persons' hand and thank them for participating in the process and for bringing their unique perspective to the forum. Then they turn to the person on the other side and do the same.

Remember...Reverence - Last, each person goes around the circle quickly and notes one thing they feel grateful for in their life. This exercise is designed to bring hope and restoration of positive energy to the group through the practice of gratitude sharing.

Staying in right relationship with self, others and the group is sacredly important

After engaging the SACRED REBOOT exercise, the facilitator returns the group back to the topical discussion to develop sacred living solutions and plans to the community challenge presented that day.

"SACRED LIVING SOLUTION CIRCLES" PARTICIPANT AGENDA AND WORKSHEET

REMINDER - Participants must remember always that we are all connected and affect each other. So, to embrace the sacred values of respect, responsibility and reverence for and toward each other at all times is our commitment; to use a sacred process that will support and benefit us and all of our brothers and sisters and planetary comrades and beings throughout the Earth.

I. Meet and Greet

a. Facilitator review of missions, goals, values, precepts, principles

b. Relationship Building Activities

1. Find one thing in common with the person asking you this question

2. Tell about something/someone that you love most in your life and why

3. Share your greatest fear in life

4. Offer one positive thing that you like about the person in your pair

5. State one thing that you are good at

6. Say something you are grateful for in your life

II. Choosing the Community Challenge

Group discussion to choose the community challenge for solution setting for that day

III. Contemplation Exercises for centering and grounding into a personal sacred space within

To start, gently contemplate your day and release the thoughts that are not positive or that cause stress by breathing them out, and then choose to release them and let them go on the out breathe. Breathe in positive energy to fill your body. Do this for 3 deep breathes in and out.

Next engage in a guided visual meditation of a sacred space at the beach. See yourself basking in the sun, feeling the wind in your hair, rubbing your toes in the sand, letting the water wash around you to help to heal and continue to relax you. Do this for another minute or 2. Next allow your imagination to remember what is sacred in your life, meaningful, valuable, full of grace, a blessing and sit in those thoughts

From this space create a sacred solution to the community challenge by contemplating on it from this more sacred place within, for a few more minutes. Write down your solution idea below...

IV. Discussion and Dialogue to Solve the community challenge
The group will determine solutions to the chosen community challenge.

Record your notes on your solution ideas as you process it in the group through consensus, collaboration and cooperative dialogue
A. Group choices for consensus building exercise

B. Group choices for Collaboration exercise

C. Group choices for Cooperation exercise

D. Don't forget to include the sacred precepts in the final solution
   do no harm, promote love to one another, look out for the planet and seven generations, benefit the greater good and weakest members

V. Celebration of Group Efforts

First... Anyone who wants to put someone in the circle for focused intent of healing does so and the group sends their love and positive energy to each other (sending love and light for the highest and most benevolent outcome).

Second... Anyone who wants to express something they celebrated this week or year in their life does so and the group shares in with their celebration energy (whistles, hoots and claps).

Third... Turn to each person next to you and give thanks to one another for participating together in the collective search for sacred living solutions to benefit the local community and or the planet as the group shares their compassion energy (shaking hands and giving hugs)) Give thanks to nature and it's life giving properties of food, air, water, plants, animals and healing energy available to and for us all of the time!!!

Fourth... Play a closing song that is inspiring, uplifting to motivate the groups sacred efforts going forward together in the circle gatherings and out in the community by sharing in celebration energy (singing, dancing)

"Remember... Follow your bliss"
- JOSEPH CAMPBELL

PERSONAL NOTES AND WORKSHEET

1. What did I learn new about myself and others at the gathering from the relationship exercise?

2. What solution did I feel most called to offer on the problem during contemplation?

3. How am I doing in implementing the 7 sacred personal values in the group discussions??
FLEXIBILITY

PATIENCE-

HUMILITY-

OPEN MIND-

HONESTY-

GRATITUDE-

KINDNESS-

4. How do I feel about the process of collaborating, finding common ground and consensus building?

5. How do I feel about the sacred reboot process and its effectiveness in managing group conflicts?

6. Write down the sacred solution plan and any way you can implement a piece of the action to include no harm, seven generations, greater good and minimal planetary impact

When a community gathers together sacredly, they create the time and space regularly for the participants to practice living in sacred relationship with one another. When they take action from this more compassionate place, they will find sacred living solutions to their shared community challenges, bonded together under the banner of unity. I do believe that, grassroots sacred communities in action all over the world can morph our planet into a place that reflects more health, peace, compassion, unconditional love and mutual support.

I have a sacred dream... of a peaceful, loving, healthy, joyous, and harmonious world where everyone has the opportunity to thrive, because Divinely empowered, compassionate, collaborative communities everywhere create and facilitate sacred living solutions to their political, economic, social, education, health challenges and needs.

Will you be part of manifesting this sacred world with me?!

Some of my group sacred leadership training that has informed my sacred living solutions process, has come from the Charter for Compassion and Life University's Center for Compassion, Integrity, and Secular Ethics, Compassionate Integrity Training Program. It is a resiliency-informed program that trains people in how to cultivate greater self-compassion and compassion for others, and to create more compassionate systems, as called for in the Charter for Compassion.

"We believe that all human beings are born with the capacity for compassion and that it must be cultivated for human beings to survive and thrive."- Charter for Compassion

Their trainings have been based on cutting-edge developments in the fields of neuroscience, psychology, trauma-informed care, peace and conflict studies, and contemplative science, and builds off of work done by Daniel Goleman (author of the book Emotional Intelligence) and Peter Senge, initiatives in Social and Emotional Learning (SEL), and others.

"By learning skills to calm our bodies and mind, becoming more emotionally aware, learning to practice compassion for ourselves and others, as well as engaging with compassion in complex systems, we can build towards compassionate integrity: the ability to live one's life in accordance with one's values with a recognition of common humanity, our basic orientation to kindness and reciprocity."- Charter for Compassion

CynThia Koloup Belden, MS, is the founder and director of Sacred Living Solutions services, spiritual life coach, mental health counselor, organizational consultant, motivational speaker and Sacred Living Solutions workshop and retreat presenter.

She currently lives in St. Augustine, Florida with her 3 rescue dogs and offers sacred living services throughout the year. She also travels around the country presenting sacred living workshops to illuminate and instruct individuals and communities on the benefits and values of implementing sacred living practices, processes and problem-solving strategies in their lives.

She is available upon request for: book signings, speaking engagements and workshops on her book, "*A CALL TO SACRED LIVING,*" and also offers support in creating "Sacred Living Solution Circles".

She also provides individual spiritual life coaching sessions in person and online to help people excavate their buried blocks to living a joyful and empowered sacred life.

CynThiaBelden@yahoo.com • 340-642-3173

Providing pathways and practices that lead
individuals and communities to
heal, transfom and thrive
in a sacred way

READING REFERENCES:

- Dr. Bruce Lipton - *The Biology of Belief*
- Dr Joe Dispenza - *You are the Placebo/Becoming Supernatural*
- Lynne McTaggart - *The Field/ The Intention Experiment/The Power of Eight*
- Dr. Sue Morter - *The Energy Codes*
- Dr. Deepak Chopra - *Quantum Healing*
- Masaru Emoto - *The Hidden Messages of Water*
- Dr Dawson Church - *Mind to Matter/ The EFT Manual*
- Ester and Jerry Hicks - *Ask and It Is Given/The Law of Attraction / The Vortex*
- Eckart Tolle - *The Power of Now*
- Heart Math Institute - *The Heart Math Solution*
- Marianne Williamson - *A Return to Love*
- Michael Singer - *The Surrender Experiment*
- Pema Chödrön - *The Places that Scare You*
- Brené Brown - *The Gifts of Imperfection*
- Dannion Brinkley - *Saved by the Light*
- Don Miguel Ruiz - *The Four Agreements*
- Alberto Villoldo - *Shaman, Healer, Sage*
- Greg Braden - *The Divine Matrix/ Walking Between the Worlds/The God Code*
- Jim Self - *Mastering Alchemy*
- *ONENESS* by Rasha
- Drunvalo Melchizedek - *Serpent of Light*
- Dr Malidoma Some - *Of Water and The Spirit/ The Healing Wisdom of Africa*
- Marlo Morgan - *Mutant Message Down Under*
- Robin Carnes - *Sacred Circles*
- Emory J Michael - *The Alchemy of Sacred Living*
- Charles Eisenstein - *Sacred Economics, The More Beautiful World Our Hearts Know is Possible*
- Kate Raworth - *Doughnut Economics*

CPSIA information can be obtained
at www.ICGtesting.com
Printed in the USA
FSHW020236110321
79283FS